6 95

DATE DUE

ELECTIONEERING IN A DEMOCRACY:

Campaigns for Congress

ELECTIONEERING IN A DEMOCRACY:

Campaigns for Congress

DAVID A. LEUTHOLD
University of Missouri

JOHN WILEY & SONS, INC.　　　New York • London • Sydney

JK1976
.L4

Copyright © 1968 by John Wiley & Sons, Inc.

All rights reserved. No part of this book may be reproduced by any means, nor transmitted, nor translated into a machine language without the written permission of the publisher.

Library of Congress Catalog Card Number: 68-22891

Printed in the United States of America

To my parents

PREFACE

Few studies are available that examine campaigns as an important process in a democratic system, or that compare campaigns from one constituency to another. This study was designed for such an examination and comparison.

The attempt to compare and contrast campaigns required the development of a conceptual framework for organizing the data. The framework used for this book is based on concepts developed originally in voting behavior studies. Because the framework emphasizes the resources needed to influence voters, it directs attention to the problem of the acquisition of those resources, a problem that is too often underestimated. The findings of this study indicate that incumbents are much more successful than their challengers in the acquisition of campaign resources, resulting in one-sided elections. This lack of meaningful competition poses potential problems for our democratic system.

I am grateful to many people and organizations for assistance in preparing this volume. Financial assistance was provided by the Research Center, School of Business and Public Administration, University of Missouri, Columbia; Falk Foundation; Institute of Governmental Studies, University of California, Berkeley; California Legislative Intern Program; Woodrow Wilson Foundation; Committee on Research, University of California; and Survey Research Center, University of California. For encouragement and helpful comments on an earlier draft, I am indebted to many people, including students in my political parties course. Any shortened list must necessarily be incomplete, but I am particularly indebted to Rondal Downing, Eugene C. Lee, David Leege, Kevin McKeough, and David Olson. William M. Reid provided valuable research assistance at a number of points. To all of these people and to many others who contributed in numerous ways, I give sincere thanks.

The cooperation of candidates, campaign managers, and campaign workers was especially appreciated. Many of them believed that a study of political campaigns would be valuable, especially to those contemplating a campaign. If this study has such value, much of the credit should be given to those political workers who contributed so willingly of their time.

The completion of the book was aided immeasurably by the encouragement, assistance, and patience of my family and, especially, my wife Carolyn.

David Leuthold

Columbia, Missouri
July, 1967

CONTENTS

1. INTRODUCTION — 1
   San Francisco Bay Area — 5
   The 1962 Election — 9

2. BECOMING A CANDIDATE — 14
   Factors Considered by Candidates — 20
   Characteristics of Attractive Candidates — 23

3. ACQUIRING PARTY SUPPORT — 32
   Primary Elections — 32
   Support of Party Leaders — 38

4. ACQUIRING ISSUE INFORMATION — 48
   Determining Voter Opinions — 48
   Search for Information on Issues — 55

5. ACQUIRING THE SUPPORT OF NON PARTY GROUPS — 61
   Value of Particular Groups — 62
   Techniques for Securing Group Support — 65
   Patterns of Support — 69

6. ACQUIRING CAMPAIGN FUNDS   **74**

    Amounts Raised   77

    Sources of Funds   78

    Procedures for Acquiring Funds   83

7. SECURING CAMPAIGN WORKERS   **86**

    Professional Campaign Workers   87

    Amateur Campaign Workers   89

8. USE OF RESOURCES – ACTIVITIES   **100**

    Measuring Activities   101

    Party, Competitiveness, Incumbency   102

9. USE OF RESOURCES – APPEALS   **112**

10. IMPLICATIONS FOR DEMOCRACY   **120**

Appendix A. List of Candidates in Bay Area Congressional Campaigns, 1962   135

Appendix B. Questionnaire Used in Survey of Campaign Workers   137

Index   141

Chapter 1

INTRODUCTION

Some concepts have such widely recognized desirability that they are given many different meanings, depending on the purposes of the user. "Democracy" is this kind of concept. Some people define democracy as social and economic justice. Others assert that it is a procedural system which may or may not produce such policies as justice. Joseph Schumpeter, a member of this group, defined democracy as "that institutional arrangement for arriving at political decisions in which individuals acquire the power to decide by means of a competitive struggle for the people's vote."[1] This definition focuses the attention of democrats on the "competitive struggle for the people's vote," particularly on election campaigns, which are the most intense form of that struggle. The amount of genuine competition in election campaigns is consequently an important measure of the meaningfulness of any democracy.

For conceptual purposes, we can consider the securing of votes as the major objective of a campaign. Not all candidates hope to win office, but the success of candidates with other purposes (such as increased business for a law practice or the dissemination of an ideology) is often indicated by the number of votes they receive. Thus, from the standpoint of the candidates, an election campaign can be considered as *the process of acquiring and using the political resources that can secure votes.* The resources that a candidate is able to acquire and the uses that he makes of them will significantly

[1] Joseph A. Schumpeter, *Capitalism, Socialism and Democracy*, third edition, Harper and Row, New York, 1962, p. 269.

determine the success of his campaign, and thus the competitiveness of the election.

Votes are secured by influencing people to favor a candidate and by insuring that people so influenced cast their ballots. Social scientists at the University of Michigan have developed a useful classification of voter attitudes, emphasizing that the decisions of voters are based on their attitudes toward four elements: the candidates, the parties, the issues, and the other groups involved in politics.[2] Each of these elements will be treated as a resource which is important for a political campaign, and which a candidate needs to acquire.

- The first element is the candidate, so that the first resource is candidacy. Acquisition of this resource involves the decision to become a candidate and the development and presentation of personal characteristics which are regarded highly by voters.
- The second resource—party—is usually acquired by winning the nomination of a major party, but it is also important to have the wholehearted support of party leaders and party organizations.
- The acquisition of the third resource—issues—requires that the candidates secure information about the attitudes of the public in order to calculate the effect of advertising particular issue positions, as well as securing information about the content of issues in order to support the stands that they adopt.
- The fourth resource is the support of normally nonpolitical groups, such as farmers, labor unions, businesses, or veterans groups.
- Two more resources—money and people—are needed in order to disseminate the information to influence public attitudes and to insure that people so influenced cast their ballots.

After some or all of these resources are acquired, the candidates employ them in an effort to secure votes. This employ-

[2]Angus Campbell, Philip E. Converse, Warren E. Miller, and Donald E. Stokes, *The American Voter*, John Wiley and Sons, New York, 1960, pp. 523–538.

ment of resources will be considered from two approaches: the types of activities used (such as advertisements, mailings, or personal contact) and the appeals that are used to influence voters.[3]

The discussion of the acquisition and use of resources will include a consideration of the effect of three factors: party (Republican or Democratic), incumbency (incumbent or nonincumbent), and competitiveness of the race (sure winner, competitive, or sure loser). These are commonly regarded as among the most important variables in political campaigns, with the contest taking place between the Republicans and Democrats, or between the "ins" and the "outs," and with greater resources usually being committed to marginal districts than to safe districts.

The data for this study came principally from the 1962 campaigns of the Republican and Democratic candidates for Congress from the ten districts that border San Francisco Bay. These campaigns were limited enough, so that a single scholar could see most of the activities of the campaign from top to bottom, in contrast to gubernatorial or senatorial campaigns which could have been viewed only in one area or on one level. Nevertheless congressional campaigns provided a contest for an office of significance to the nation, and one in which the national as well as the local parties took interest,

[3]Many of the previous studies of campaigns have emphasized the concept of strategy, which V. O. Key, Jr. defined as a general plan which "may fix the principal propaganda themes to be emphasized in the campaign, define the chief targets within the electorate, schedule the peak output of effort, and set other broad features of the campaign." *Politics, Parties and Pressure Groups*, fifth edition, Thomas Y. Crowell, New York, 1964, p. 462. Most discussions of strategy have been based, implicitly or explicitly, on presidential or other high level competitive races in which appearances indicate that the candidate has been freed from many of the problems of acquiring resources. The framework for this study suggests, however, that strategy should be defined as an overall plan for acquiring and using the resources needed for a campaign. The findings for this study will indicate that the problems of acquisition are more significant than the problems of using the resources. As a result, the decision on making an appeal for the labor vote, for example, will depend not only on the proportion of the constituency which is labor-oriented, but also on the success that the candidate has had in acquiring such resources as the support of labor leaders, the money and workers needed to send a mailing to labor union members, and information about issues important to labor people.

4   Introduction

so that there was some activity in almost every campaign. In contrast, many of the campaigns for the state legislature and local office were comparatively one-sided and contained only limited activity. In addition, the numerous publications on Congress and congressional behavior provided much more background information than is available for most offices. The 10 congressional districts that border on San Francisco Bay and the 20 campaigns in these districts provided a large enough number for evaluation of the effect of various factors. The particular location of the districts, however, means that the findings are more applicable to the personal, candidate-oriented politics of the western United States than to the organizational, party-oriented politics of the East.[4]

The principal sources of information for this study included the following ones.

- Observation of candidates and campaign events in 19 of the 20 campaigns.
- Interviews with candidates, campaign managers, and key workers.
- Literature and advertisements used in each campaign.
- Responses to a two-page mail questionnaire sent to workers in the campaigns.
- Financial reports submitted from each campaign to the California Secretary of State.

In this study, competitiveness was estimated on the basis of evaluations of the party registration of the constituency, past vote results, and the campaigns conducted by the candidates, assessing in the period shortly before election day whether each of two opposing candidates had some reasonable prospect of winning. The relative accuracy of the judgments was substantiated on election day when all candidates who were judged sure winners received 60 percent or more of the vote while candidates who were considered competitive received 40 to 60 percent of the vote.

[4]For an excellent description of congressional politics in Chicago, an area where political machines are significant, see Leo M. Snowiss, "Congressional Recruitment and Representation," *American Political Science Review*, **60**, 627–639 (1966).

FIGURE 1. MAP OF THE TEN CONGRESSIONAL DISTRICTS IN THE SAN FRANCISCO BAY AREA, 1962

SAN FRANCISCO BAY AREA

The ten congressional districts covered in this study all touched on San Francisco Bay, although two of them extended quite far north, one as far as the Oregon border (see Figure 1). The area of these ten districts was approximately the same as that of West Virginia, and the population was approximately the same as that of Wisconsin, Virginia, or Georgia.

The economy of the region was highly diversified with manufacturing, trade, professional services, agriculture, and lumbering all being important. No single industry was dominant, but those considered particularly significant by local people included shipping, finance and insurance, defense work, lumber, education, and agriculture.

The population of the 10 districts was comparatively prosperous and well educated. Median family income in 1959 was about $7000 in the region compared to about $4800 for the United States. The median educational level of adults in 1960 was over 12 years of school for the Bay Area compared to 10.6 for the United States.[5] These characteristics are relevant for election campaigns, because well-educated and high-income people participate more than people with less education or income.

California and the Bay Area have had a unique political history, one shaped especially by the Progressives of the early 20th century.[6] In California this group of young professionals and small businessmen successfully fought the Southern Pacific railroad and elected Hiram Johnson as governor in 1910. The Progressives were strong individualists, and one of their principal tenets was opposition to the big bureaucracies — the big corporations, the big unions, and even the big political parties. Strict controls were established over big bureaucracy in each of its forms — the restrictions on the political parties rendered them largely ineffective. The Progressives established nonpartisan elections for all units of local government and for judicial offices. They established the system of cross-filing, whereby all tests of party loyalty for candidates were eliminated and a candidate might campaign

[5]For an extensive analysis of this region, see David Leuthold, "Electioneering in a Democracy: Congressional Election Campaigns in the San Francisco Bay Area 1962," unpublished Ph.D. dissertation, University of California, Berkeley, 1965, pp. 10–14, 299–305.
[6]This discussion relies heavily on George E. Mowry, *The California Progressives*, University of California Press, Berkeley, 1951.

for and win the nomination of more than one party. Candidates gradually learned that the most effective appeals under cross-filing were nonpartisan appeals, and that incumbents could often win the nominations of both parties in the primary. The Progressives undermined party leadership through the introduction of the referendum, initiative, and recall. They eliminated many of the rewards that the party could offer by establishing an effective nonpartisan civil service, which corresponded with their concepts of moralism, professionalism, and nonpartisanship. Having talent and personality, the Progressives argued that these traits should be the dominant considerations in the selection of public officials rather than riches or the organizational qualities (such as patience) required by bureaucratic political parties.

While Governor Hiram Johnson was in office, he ran an effective political machine based largely upon personal loyalty. His election to the U.S. Senate in 1916 left a power vacuum, into which stepped a large number of pressure groups, including agriculture, liquor, labor, pensioners and would-be pensioners, teachers, and the railroads. Local newspapers became significant factors in political campaigns. With the stabilizing and rationalizing influence of major party responsibility removed, California also proved hospitable to a number of extremist and Utopian groups including Upton Sinclair's EPIC, Technocracy, the Townsend Plan, Ham and Eggs, the Communist party, and the John Birch society. The rise of these groups, the emphasis on personality, and the antiparty bureaucracy attitudes allowed men to rise quickly to the top without seasoning experience. The absence of party professionals as campaign advisors and managers encouraged the growth of public relations and campaign management firms that operated behind the scenes.

The relative ineffectiveness of parties and the emphasis on nonpartisanship meant that shifts in party support became much more acceptable, so that in each campaign there were a number of personal endorsements of Republican candidates by "life-long Democrats" and vice versa. This lack of party loyalty also meant greater support of third parties by California voters than by United States voters, as indicated by the following votes for third parties:[7]

Party and Year	Percent of Total Vote Received in:	
	California	United States
Progressives, 1912	42	27
Progressives, 1924	33	17
Independent Progressives, 1948	5	2

Changes in the 1950's

This picture of strong pressure groups, ineffective parties, and personality politics changed sharply in the 1950's. In 1950 the power of pressure groups was reduced by lobbying laws designed especially to curb the activities of Artie Samish, noted lobbyist for many groups. The effectiveness of the Democratic party was increased by the formation, in 1953, of the California Democratic Council, a statewide volunteer organization, whose members were able and willing to provide the manpower needed for effective campaigns. Prior to that, Republican candidates, relying on their personal organizations, had dominated state politics. The most notable of these Republicans, Governor Earl Warren, left state politics in 1953 when he was appointed Chief Justice of the United States Supreme Court. A 1954 law reduced the effect of personality by listing the party affiliation of candidates on the primary ballot, a step that weakened cross-filing and helped lead to its abolition in 1959. As a result of these changes California had, by 1962, much stronger political parties than it had before 1950.

Nevertheless in 1962 the formal party organizations were still hampered by restrictive laws that prohibited continuing

[7]Svend Petersen, *A Statistical History of the American Presidential Elections*, Ungar Press, New York, 1963, pp. 116, 121. The proportion of California's vote given to the 1912 Progressives was probably increased by the fact that California Governor Hiram Johnson was the candidate for Vice-President on that ticket. However, in 1948, California Governor Earl Warren was candidate for Vice-President on the Republican ticket, but the vote for the Independent Progressives was still higher than for the nation as a whole. All three of these Progressive parties were more liberal than the two national parties.

leadership and that provided different bases of support for the state and local parties. The informal organizations, however, were active and effective. The most important volunteer groups were the California Republican Assembly and the California Democratic Council, each of which was formed after its party had lost control of the national government—the CRA in 1934 and the CDC in 1953. Both organizations regularly recruited and endorsed candidates and helped provide campaign support. Also, the California Democratic Council took stands on many issues.

THE 1962 ELECTION

The election campaigns in California in 1962 were notable especially for the attempt of Richard Nixon to make a political comeback by running for the office of governor, and for the counterattempt of Edmund (Pat) Brown to be the first Democratic governor reelected to office in more than a century.[8] The gubernatorial contest was concerned especially with state issues, and its main effect on the congressional campaigns was to establish an atmosphere of competition and interest. There was also distinct public interest in the state-level campaigns for superintendent of public instruction and for and against ballot proposition 24, a purported anti-Communist proposal that was defeated.[9] Only limited interest was stimulated by the U.S. Senate race in which Thomas Kuchel easily won reelection over State Senator Richard Richards from Los Angeles County. With but minor exceptions the congressional candidates ignored the statewide campaigns except as they were required or hoped to share workers, finances, and advertising.

---

[8]For an analysis of the election, see Totton J. Anderson and Eugene C. Lee, "The 1962 Election in California," *Western Political Quarterly*, 16, 396–420 (1963).
[9]For an analysis of voting behavior on this issue, see Jenniellen W. Ferguson and Paul J. Hoffman, "Voting Behavior: The Vote on the Francis Amendment in the 1962 California Election," *Western Political Quarterly*, 17, 770–776 (1964).

Bay Area Campaigns

Between 1950 and 1960 the Bay Area gained sufficient population to justify two new congressional seats and the 1961 legislature drew new boundary lines for all Bay Area congressional districts except one. In several districts the changes were minor, involving only a reduction in the size of the district so that congressmen had no new constituents. Nevertheless, the changes of boundary lines unsettled political expectations sufficiently, so that there was more competition for office than normal.

In addition, the 1962 Bay Area congressional campaigns were affected by several October events. The length of the congressional session, extending into the middle of October, restricted the campaign activities of most incumbents, and thus depressed activity and interest in the campaigns because no debate was possible until the incumbents returned. The length of the session also forced the cancellation of then-Senator Hubert Humphrey's speaking tour in which he had intended to endorse several Bay Area nonincumbents.

Interest in the 1962 election was also reduced by the World Series. The San Francisco Giants tied the Los Angeles Dodgers on the last day of the regular baseball season, defeated them in a three-game playoff, and narrowly lost to the New York Yankees in a seven-game World Series which was lengthened by postponements. Needless to say, the Bay Area was temporarily excited about baseball, and candidates found that many of their workers, advertising agents, and associates were either attending the games or watching them on television.

The political partisanship of Bay Area campaigns was reduced by the Cuban missile crisis which started on October 22. Most of the incumbents subsequently used their political speeches for explanations of the crisis situation and for requests for support of the government, thus illustrating their familiarity with the problems of the world and, for Republicans, their nonpartisanship. The three congressmen who served on the Armed Services and Foreign Affairs Committees referred discreetly but frequently to the secret briefings that they had received in Washington in September. (All of the incumbent congressmen received a secret briefing in San Francisco a few days after the crisis broke.) Political trips to the Bay Area by President Kennedy and Commerce Secretary Luther Hodges were cancelled because of the missile crisis.

Most of the 20 campaigns covered in this study were exciting, but the diversity of names and events would be difficult to keep straight if all were reported. (A complete list of candidates is included in Appendix A.) Consequently 2 contests will be used as illustrations, although generalized conclusions will be based on all 10 districts. The 2 contests were in the Fourth District, a newly reapportioned district without an incumbent, and the Sixth District, a competitive contest in which a major effort was made to unseat an incumbent. Each contest deserves a brief summary.

Fourth District (Competitive, No Incumbent). The Democratic-controlled state legislature drew the lines of the new Fourth District to insure a Democratic victory. Republicans, nevertheless, were hopeful because the largest county in the district had given a majority in the three previous elections to the moderate Republican congressman whose district it had then included. The district was predominantly agricultural, but it did include many government workers from Mare Island Naval Shipyard and from Travis Air Force Base.

The Democratic candidate was Assemblyman (State Representative) Robert Leggett, a young lawyer who had been first elected to the California Assembly just 2 years before. Leggett started campaigning for Congress in July 1961, and won the primary after a bruising and expensive campaign against Assemblyman Lloyd Lowrey, who had represented another part of the congressional district for 22 years. In the general election, Leggett was supported by many young professional and business friends and generally by Democrats throughout the district, although some of the liberals feared that he was too compromising and too "ambitious." Much of the financing for the campaign was provided by Leggett and his personal friends and associates.

The Republicans convinced Admiral L. V. "Mike" Honsinger, commanding officer of the Mare Island Naval Shipyard, to run for the office. Honsinger was inexperienced in campaign politics, but he was respected by the shipyard employees, and he had appeared more than 100 times before congressional committees as a spokesman for the Navy. Many party workers enthusiastically supported him. A number of Democratic workers indicated that they would have supported him also, if Honsinger's political and economic views had not been so conservative. Financing for his campaign came largely from the Republican organization, which proved less organized and competent than Honsinger had hoped. Leggett won the election with about 56 percent of the vote.

Sixth District (Competitive, Incumbent). The Sixth District, which covered much of the residential and industrial area of San Francisco, was enlarged during the 1961 reapportionment, increasing the Democratic percentage of two-party registration by several percentage points. The incumbent was moderate Republican William Mailliard, who won his seat by defeating the Democratic incumbent in 1952. (Mailliard had lost a close race to the same incumbent in 1948.) A member of a socially prominent San Francisco family, Mailliard had held various banking and semipublic positions before his election to Congress, and had served as secretary to Governor Earl Warren. In Congress he had concentrated his attention on shipping and the merchant marine, and also on foreign affairs after his 1961 appointment to that committee.

His challenger was California Assemblyman John O'Connell. O'Connell had served for a number of years as a freight forwarder, then had attended evening law school. In 1954, shortly after his graduation, he had been elected to the county central committee, largely on the basis of his Irish name and occupation. As one of the participants in a struggle for power on the committee that year, O'Connell had been selected as the Democratic nominee for the State Assembly in a safely Democratic district after the voters had renominated the incumbent, despite the incumbent's death just before the primary. Thereafter, O'Connell had little or no opposition for reelection. He was one of the most liberal members of the Assembly, displaying special concern about civil rights and social welfare measures.

O'Connell easily won the congressional primary, defeating the chairman of the San Francisco Democratic County Central Committee. He put on a vigorous general election campaign, receiving strong support from liberals, peace groups, labor unions, and college students. Many of his workers came from the East Bay (Berkeley-Oakland), while much of his financial support came from southern California. Much of O'Connell's campaign time was spent ringing doorbells and visiting outlying merchants, emphasizing his links with President Kennedy, Governor Brown, and other official Democratic candidates.

Mailliard, who was unopposed in the primary, ran an extensive campaign that relied especially upon the proven workers, managers and contributors of previous years. He secured the public support of the metropolitan newspapers and of a number of prominent Democrats who appreciated Mailliard's liberalism and support of shipping interests, and feared O'Connell's "radicalism." Mailliard made numerous personal appearances, asking for support on the basis of his record. He won the election with about 58 percent of the vote.

For these 4 candidates, and for the other 16, the success of their campaigns depended, first, on the acquisition of resources and, second, on their use of these resources. The next 4 chapters will discuss the acquisition of the campaign resources of candidacy, party, issues, and groups.

Chapter 2

BECOMING A CANDIDATE

The relative importance of each of the four campaign resources was indicated by responses of voters, when asked in national surveys in 1960 and 1962 for the "most important reason" for their voting decision in their district's congressional race.[1] If voters had a second reason, it was coded also. The reasons given were classified into one of the four campaign resources categories or a miscellaneous category. The proportion of *reasons* in each category was:

	1960 (Percent)	1962 (Percent)
Candidate	40	44
Party	47	31
Issues	5	13
Group	3	5
Other (influence of relatives, etc.)	5	7
Total	100	100
Number of reasons	(1331)	(804)

The resources of candidate and party are obviously mentioned quite often; those of issues and group are mentioned less often.

The importance of the candidate indicates that the first question that should be asked is "How is the candidate acquired?" or, in other words, "What is the process by which a

---

[1] Data from fall 1960 and fall 1962 omnibus surveys collected and prepared by Survey Research Center, University of Michigan, and made available by the Inter-university Consortium for Political Research. Neither organization is responsible for the analyses or interpretations.

man decides to become a candidate?" After he has decided to run, the next question is "What are his personal characteristics, and which of these should he emphasize in the campaign?" (An additional question that future researchers should ask is "Do candidates intentionally develop those characteristics desired by the voters, and if so, what is the process?" The relevance of the question was not realized until after the data had been gathered for this study.[2])

The characteristics of candidates which voters mention will not be the only important ones. Other significant characteristics will include the amount of money the candidate can contribute to his campaign, the number of volunteer workers he can secure, the groups and party leaders from which he can win support, and the issue information and viewpoints he has. These other characteristics will be considered in subsequent chapters however, and this chapter will be restricted to a consideration of characteristics noted by voters.

Some men find politics or a legislative body so fascinating that they are drawn irresistibly to candidacy; other men find business or fishing or something else exciting, and become candidates only as a result of someone else's strong urging. Previous studies of state legislators and legislative candidates have reported widely varying percentages of "self-starters" and "recruits", with the median study reporting that about 50 percent of the candidates fell into each group. Those who said that they had been recruited mentioned party leaders most frequently as the recruiting agents, followed by friends and associates. Interest group representatives were credited with suggesting very few candidacies.[3] Some researchers

---

[2]In his novels, Eugene Burdick makes it clear that he believes that such a process exists. See *The Ninth Wave*, Houghton Mifflin, Boston, 1956, p. 235, and *The 480*, McGraw-Hill, New York, 1964, p. 11. The only applicable Bay Area data were the comments by a number of long-time workers for one congressman. These people noted that he had originally been retiring and even antisocial, a sensitive individual who found it difficult to mix with people. When he became involved in politics, he trained himself to become a good mixer and to engage in social affairs.

[3]See Frank J. Sorauf, *Party and Representation: Legislative Politics in Pennsylvania*, Atherton Press, New York, 1963, pp. 102–103; David M. Olson, *Legislative Primary Elections in Austin, Texas, 1962*, Public Affairs Series No. 54, Institute of Public Affairs, University of Texas, *(continued)*,

have noted however that this dichotomy between self-starters and recruits seemed artificial. For example, Frank Sorauf has pointed out that:[4]

> The issue of the self-starting candidacy is . . . complex. . . . Under the flattering stimulus of party hints and overtures, the candidate-to-be may develop ambitions or may at least make the party's will his own. By the same token, he may become the object of party encouragement only after he has carefully hinted his availability or his contemplation of a candidacy.

This complexity was clearly evident in the Bay Area. Most nonincumbents could be classified as either self-starters or recruits. Only 1 of the 12 was not at least partially a self-starter, and only 4 were not influenced by party leaders. Some of these candidates were also influenced by interest group leaders. One of the reasons for difficulty in assigning classifications was that some individuals played more than one role; for example, in one district a county central committee chairman decided to run, leaving the political scientists with the problem of classifying him either as a self-starter or as a candidate recruited by a party leader (himself) or as both. In another district the party leader most active in the recruiting process was a leader of lumber and timber

---

Austin, 1963 p. 16; Lester Seligman, "A Prefatory Study of Leadership Selection in Oregon," *Western Political Quarterly*, 12, 162 (1959); John C. Wahlke, Heinz Eulau, William Buchanan, and LeRoy C. Ferguson, *The Legislative System: Explorations in Legislative Behavior*, John Wiley and Sons, New York, 1962, pp. 98–100. For a table comparing the findings of these studies, see David A. Leuthold, "Electioneering in a Democracy: Congressional Election Campaigns in The San Francisco Bay Area 1962," unpublished Ph.D. dissertation, University of California, Berkeley, 1965, p. 41.

One difficulty in the use of the term "self-starter" is that two different meanings are applied to it: candidates who decided to run without being urged, or without much urging from others, and candidates who were weak and had few prospects of winning, although they may or may not have been urged by others to run. For an example of usage of the first definition, see Sorauf, *op. cit.*, p. 102. For usage of the second, see Seligman, *op. cit.*, pp. 162–163; Lester Seligman, "Political Recruitment and Party Structure: A Case Study," *American Political Science Review*, 55, 85 (1961); Leonard Rowe and William Buchanan, "Campaign Funds in California: What the Records Reveal," *California Historical Society Quarterly*, 41, 200, 207 (1962); and Charles G. Mayo, "The 1961 Mayoralty Election in Los Angeles: The Political Party in a Nonpartisan Election," *Western Political Quarterly*, 17, 331 (1964).

[4]Sorauf, *op. cit.*, p. 103.

groups, so that his candidate could have been classified as the recruit of either the party or an interest group. Generally the classifications seemed to be meaningless, because most candidacies were the happy combination of a candidate who had wanted to run for some office and of party or interest group leaders who wanted the strongest congressional candidate they could find. Perhaps a case study in the Fourth District will help to give the flavor of the process.

The new Fourth Congressional District, solidly Democratic in registration, was reportedly established for Democratic Assemblyman Lloyd Lowrey, a farmer who had served in the legislature for 22 years, and Lowrey filed for the office. The district included, however, the home of another Democratic Assemblyman, Robert Leggett, a young attorney who was serving his first term in the legislature. After a number of discussions with people who had worked closely with him in his 1960 campaign, Leggett decided that if he were going to make a career of politics, he should take this opportunity to run for Congress. A third candidate, also from Leggett's home area, wanted to run, although he and Leggett realized that the split of the local vote would give the election to Lowrey. Since neither wished to withdraw, they "agreed" that each should campaign hard and see what happened. After a couple of months of campaigning, the third candidate withdrew from the race, accepting a judgeship which he had been offered. The California Democratic Council declined to choose between Leggett and Lowrey and made no endorsement.[5] The party officials in the district generally gave their support to the Assemblyman who had represented their part of the district. Leggett won a close primary election in which each Assemblyman got a very large majority in his own part of the district. In this example the candidate (Leggett) was a self-starter and party leader, who made his decision only after numerous discussions with business associates and political friends.

Candidate-recruiting committees, where they existed, were

[5]One reason for the refusal may have been that the CDC was not enthusiastic about either candidate, a not unusual situation, for many CDC members seemed suspicious of elected officeholders and the compromises to which they agreed in order to be effective.

often likely to choose simply among those candidates who presented themselves, although they might well have tried earlier to recruit stronger candidates. In such cases the committees usually saw the candidates as self-starters asking for support, while the candidates considered themselves as recruits, noting that they would not have run except for the encouragement they received from the committee. For example, in one district the minority party recruiting committee tried to recruit a Congressional Medal of Honor winner, going so far as to ask an industrial company to put him on its payroll during the campaign. The company declined to do so, and the prospective candidate decided not to run. A local elected official indicated interest, but told the committee he would make his decision without reference to the committee's desires or endorsement. The committee was willing to support him, believing him to be a strong candidate, but he decided that he could not win. Finally the committee made a public call for prospective candidates, interviewed the seven who arrived, and decided on one whose employer had already agreed to contribute heavily to the campaign expenses.

This example indicates that the prestige of a potentially losing congressional candidacy is not high enough to attract the strongest candidates, but it is attractive to some people. In addition, the congressional district power structures, at least in California, are fluid. Consequently, in most districts a large number of people consider themselves prospective candidates, and another large group of people consider themselves prospective recruiters. The potential number of recruiters was indicated in the 1952 election in the Eleventh District. Republican leaders in that district decided to open membership on the candidate-recruiting committee to any and all Republicans who wished to join. Eventually 312 people became members. The number of prospective candidates was indicated by the unusual situation in the First District, where campaigning Congressman Clem Miller was killed in an airplane crash in mid-October 1962. Local Democratic party leaders decided not to select a write-in candidate, but to continue to ask for votes for Miller in the hope that he would be elected, thus requiring a special election for which the party would be better prepared.[6] From the day of Miller's death until election day, party officials remained publicly silent on any possible candidacies because unity was needed, for there would have been no special election if Miller had not won the November election. Nevertheless the party headquarters received calls or letters suggesting 47 different people as the Democratic candidate for the prospective special election. At least 10 people publicly indicated interest in running.

The number of prospective candidates and of candidate-recruiters depended somewhat on the chances for success. The 312-member committee and the 47 prospective candidates were in districts in which the party's candidate could hope to do well. In districts that a party was sure to lose, significantly fewer people thought of themselves as candidates. In district-parties represented already by an incumbent there was little maneuvering, unless the incumbent was elderly and near retirement. The number of candidates who filed, even in districts that the party was sure to lose, indicated that congressional nominations in themselves were prestigious enough to attract candidates. This is apparently not true of nominations for the state legislature because previous studies have reported that party leaders are often forced to recruit candidates in those state legislative districts that they are sure to lose.[7]

Party leaders became involved sooner or later in most cases. The original impetus may have come from the candidate, from friends or associates, or from an interest group, but the decision to continue the candidacy or withdraw often depended upon the attitude of party leaders. In the 10 districts, 13 men filed as candidates for the primary, knowing

[6]The strategy was successful in that Miller was elected by a narrow margin. However the Republican loser ran again in the special election and won, defeating Miller's administrative assistant.
[7]Sorauf, *op. cit.*, p. 103. See also Seligman, "Political Recruitment and Party Structure," *op. cit.*, p. 84; Olson, *op. cit.*, p. 16; and Charles B. Judah and Dorothy P. Goldberg, *The Recruitment of Candidates from Bernalillo County to the New Mexico House of Representatives, 1956*, Division of Research, Department of Government, University of New Mexico, Albuquerque, 1959.

that some party leaders had already committed themselves to another candidate; only 3 of the 13 won a primary nomination. Official Republican leaders appeared to be more active and more directly involved in the recruiting process than Democratic officials. Despite their reputation as recruiters, neither the California Republican Assembly nor the California Democratic Council was especially active in recruiting candidates.

FACTORS CONSIDERED BY CANDIDATES

Because the dichotomy between self-starters and recruits seems awkward, a more fruitful approach to this topic of becoming a candidate is to ask, "What are the factors a man considers when he decides to become a candidate?" Some answers have been provided by studies asking congressmen and legislators (1) how they became candidates, (2) whether or not they intend to run for reelection and why, or (3) whether or not they intend to run for another office.[8] Generally these studies have indicated that the important considerations, roughly in order, have been the following ones.

1. Personal political considerations: the degree of the candidate's commitment to politics, his desire for a political career and his involvement in his present political position; the likelihood of winning, the amount of support available, and the strength of opposition that can be expected; the degree of commitment that the candidate has to public service, and the strength of his feeling of obligation to his community, or the strength of his desire to help his district.

2. Economic considerations: the effect that candidacy and officeholding will have on the candidate's income, and the

[8]Wahlke *et al., op. cit.*, pp. 121–134; Charles L. Clapp, *The Congressman: His Work As He Sees It*, Brookings Institution, Washington, D.C., 1963, pp. 31–34; Olson, *op cit.*, pp. 11–15; Sorauf, *op. cit.*, pp. 98–101; Robert M. Rosenzweig, "The Politician and the Career in Politics," *Midwest Journal of Political Science*, 1, 166 (1957); Judah and Goldberg, *op. cit.*, p. 17. See also the reasons given by Congressmen for retirement from Congress, *Congressional Quarterly Weekly Report*, September 28, 1962, pp. 1741–1742, and March 4, 1966, pp. 502–503.

extent to which they will advance or hinder his nonpolitical career; the attitude of the candidate's employer and the possibility that he may be forced to find a new job.

3. Family and other personal considerations: the extent to which the candidate's family approves of his candidacy and is willing to assist in the campaign; the health and energy of the candidate and his ability to undertake the strain of the campaign; the extent to which the candidate will gain or lose social prestige by running or by being elected.

4. Dissatisfaction by the prospective candidate with the incumbent, the possible opponent, or the other party.

5. Issue or group orientation: desire to pass some specific legislation.

6. Desire to help the party: this consideration is usually pertinent only if the candidate would be a sacrificial candidate.

There are some indications in the studies that candidates occasionally make provisional decisions, deciding tentatively to run but being willing to back out if sufficient support is not received or if strong opposition develops. Much more frequently, however, the studies indicate that candidates decide to run and then go looking for support, often staying in the race even though they fail to receive the degree of support that they had wanted.

The fourth and sixth factors listed—dissatisfaction with the incumbent and desire to help the party—indicate the most significant differences that have been reported among types of candidates. Interviews with winners and losers of legislative contests in Pennsylvania indicated that losers mentioned dissatisfaction with the incumbent and a desire to help the district, while winners spoke of their interest in politics and public affairs and their feeling of obligation for public service. Similarly, studies in New Mexico and Texas reported that it was minority party candidates who specified that they wished to aid their party. In contrast, differences in the reasons given by Republicans and Democrats appear to be negligible, judged by the interviews in Pennsylvania.[9]

[9] Sorauf, *op. cit.*, pp. 99, 101; Olson, *op. cit.*, p. 14; Judah and Goldberg, *op. cit.*, p. 17.

In the Bay Area, almost all of the candidates and prospective candidates seemed quite desirous of the prestige and power accorded to congressmen and congressional candidates, but significant differences appeared between the experienced and inexperienced candidates on other considerations, judging experience by such factors as previous officeholding, and previous campaigning.

Experienced candidates gave much more serious and accurate consideration to their chances of winning. Inexperienced candidates often did not realize that they had no chance of winning. After the election, one candidate noted with chagrin that he had not learned until after he had lost that no candidate of his party could hope to win in a district in which registration so overwhelmingly favored the opposite party. One Democratic candidate checked precinct totals and found that in 1958 Democratic Governor Edmund Brown carried the area which was now his district. From this information he concluded that he could win by staying even with the Governor. He overlooked or did not weigh appropriately the facts that 1958, a year of Democratic triumphs across the nation, was not likely to be repeated, and that the Democratic congressional candidate in 1958 had not been able to stay even with the Governor. Fourth District Republican L. V. "Mike" Honsinger decided to run after receiving promises from party leaders that their organizations would support him; during the campaign he found that many of the organizations were empty shells. The evaluations of experienced candidates were usually more accurate. For example, two experienced men who were offered nominations decided after investigation to run for other offices where they would have a better chance of winning. However, one indication that even inexperienced candidates had reasonable evaluations of the prospects was that many more candidates, experienced and inexperienced, put themselves forward in those districts in which their party was competitive than in those districts the party was sure to lose.

Inexperienced candidates gave less complete consideration than experienced candidates to the economic effects of running, usually considering only the effect that winning would have on their economic situation and ignoring the effect of the campaign. Several of the inexperienced candidates had expected to run a second time if they lost the first time, but had not realized that they would still be paying the debts of the first campaign when time for the second one came around. Experienced candidates were admittedly not as likely to go into debt, but they were also more realistic about the possibility of incurring campaign debts.

Inexperienced candidates had little basis for estimating the effects that the campaigns would have on their family life and their health. Most families had given their consent to the campaigns, but some, finding the campaigns distasteful and burdensome, gradually withdrew, objecting to the reduction of time for family activities. Other families participated more and more as the campaign progressed. Similarly, the physical and emotional strains affected the health of some candidates. One was hospitalized shortly before the election and another, weakened by the campaign, died of illness 6 months after the election.

The differences between experienced and inexperienced candidates were often the differences between incumbents and nonincumbents. Incumbents had run before, and they could predict accurately their chances of winning and the economic and personal effects of the campaign. The nonincumbents were largely inexperienced, 7 of the 12 nonincumbents not having run for public office before, and 3 of the 5 with previous campaign experience having run only for a local office with a restricted constituency.

CHARACTERISTICS OF ATTRACTIVE CANDIDATES

An answer to the second question—the personal characteristics that a candidate should emphasize in his campaign—requires data about the characteristics that voters consider desirable in a candidate. Little research has been conducted on this question, but such evidence as is available indicates that voters have looked first for indicators of the candidate's ability to perform the duties of office satisfactorily and, second, for some evidence that the candidate would represent them, that is, that he had a concern for their problems or that he was similar enough to them so that he had the same problems. There are also some indications that voters gave greater attention to ability to perform the duties of the office when considering candidates for higher level office, and relatively more attention to the representativeness of the candidate—his similarity in ethnic background, religion, place of residence—when considering candidates for lower level office.

The evidence that is available comes from several opinion polls and surveys in which voters were asked what qualities they desired in political candidates, or what they liked or disliked about particular candidates.[10] The categories in these surveys are not always comparable, nor are the results always similar, but generally the qualities emphasized by voters, in order of importance, were:

Most important characteristic
 Experience
Next most important characteristics
 Honesty, integrity

[10]See Ray C. Bliss, "The Role of the State Chairman," *Politics U.S.A.: A Practical Guide to the Winning of Public Office*, James M. Cannon, ed., Doubleday, Garden City, New York, 1960, p. 165; Jerome S. Bruner and Sheldon J. Korchin, "The Boss and the Vote: A Case Study in City Politics," *Public Opinion Quarterly*, 10, 14 (1946); Angus Campbell, Philip E. Converse, Warren E. Miller, and Donald E. Stokes, *The American Voter*, John Wiley and Sons, New York, 1960, pp. 55–58; Lewis A. Dexter, "More on Voters' Information About Candidates," *PROD (Political Research: Organization and Design)*, 1, 37–38 (1958); Ernest Havemann, "People's Choice for L.B.J.'s V.P.: A *Life* Poll by Elmo Roper," *Life*, 57, 68–73 (August 14, 1964); Murray B. Levin, *The Alienated Voter: Politics in Boston*, Holt, Rinehart and Winston, New York, 1960, pp. 37–43; Murray B. Levin, *The Compleat Politician: Political Strategy in Massachusetts*, Bobbs-Merrill, Indianapolis, 1962, pp. 127–130; and Robert E. Riggs, "The District Five Primary—A Case Study in Practical Politics," *Arizona Review of Business and Public Administration*, 12, 9 (March 1963). For a summary listing of the results of these surveys, see Leuthold, *op. cit.*, pp. 306–311. David Leege surveyed delegates to the Indiana Democratic convention and found that they looked for similar characteristics when nominating candidates for statewide office. "The Place of the Party Nominating Convention in a Representative Democracy: A Study of Power in the Indiana Democratic Party's State Nominating Conventions, 1956–62," Unpublished Ph. D. dissertation, Indiana University, Bloomington, 1965, pp. 186–187.

Education, intelligence
Frequently mentioned characteristics
Independence, decisiveness
Leadership, administrative ability
Aggressiveness, strength
Youth, energy, good health
Nice personality
Sincerity
Family man, good family life (not divorced)
Occasionally mentioned characteristics (some
of which overlap those given above)
Speaking ability
Nationality or race
Concern for the problems of the people
Sense of duty and patriotism
Reliability and trustworthiness
Efficiency
Good financial and business background
Courage
Military service

Although not specifically mentioned in these surveys, other surveys have indicated that voters prefer men more than women.[11]

Voters also mentioned frequently the importance of knowing about the candidate's characteristics and, in many cases, they have indicated that their reason for voting for a candidate was that they were acquainted with him. In the 1960 SRC national survey, about 5 percent of the voters mentioned personal contact with or knowledge about the congressional candidate as their most important reason for voting for him. This would be equivalent to 3000 to 5000 votes for winning candidates.[12] The total number of votes for a "personal friend" has been estimated at 10,000 to 15,000 for single candidates in Boston mayoralty elections.[13] Probably at least

[11]Hadley Cantril, ed., *Public Opinion 1935-1946*, Princeton University Press, Princeton, 1951, pp. 134, 1052-1054.
[12]Data made available by the Inter-university Consortium for Political Research.
[13]Bruner and Korchin, op. cit., pp. 16-17; Levin, *The Alienated Voter*, op. cit., pp. 37-38.

some of these friendships were presumed by the voter after a chance meeting or the receipt of campaign literature, but nevertheless a significant number of votes have been cast for "personal friends."

Generally voters are more willing to vote for a person whom they have heard of (or whom they think they have heard of) than for a person whom they have never heard of. (This fact helps to explain the vote-getting ability of movie stars.) One Boston survey found that candidates for mayor finished in the same order in the election as the order in which respondents had been able to identify their names in a preelection survey.[14] Another survey showed that one third of a candidate's votes were received because voters identified him with a similarly named, well-respected relative.[15] A name may be well known for several reasons, including the establishment of a reputation in public service, elective positions, or business, or the acquiring of popularity as an entertainment figure, sports star, or military hero. This reputation or popularity may be established by the candidate, a relative or ancestor or, unfortunately in some cases, by a nonrelative with the same family name. Examples of capitalizing on the popular names of others have been reported in Detroit city elections, where good "names" have been significant enough so that some would-be candidates have dropped their family names for more popular ones such as Roosevelt or Murphy. Similarly, in Massachusetts elections, various Kennedys capitalized on the popularity of John F. Kennedy, with an unrelated John F. Kennedy being elected state treasurer.[16]

Because voters have considered ability to perform the duties of office very significant and have looked specifically

[14]Bruner and Korchin, *op. cit.*, p. 17.
[15]Riggs, *op. cit.*, p. 9.
[16]Maurice M. Ramsey, *Name Candidates in Detroit Elections*, Detroit Bureau of Governmental Research, Detroit, 1941, p. 9; Levin, *The Compleat Politician, op. cit.*, pp. 42–43. A 1964 survey in Boone County, Missouri, site of the University of Missouri, revealed that 67 percent of the respondents could accurately identify Dan Devine, the University's football coach, but only 30 percent could identify Richard Ichord, the local congressman. The survey was conducted by the Public Opinion Survey Unit, Research Center, School of Business and Public Administration, University of Missouri.

at experience as an indicator of this ability, incumbents, having held the office, have had distinct advantages over nonincumbents. In addition, the names of incumbents were usually much more widely known than the names of nonincumbents.

The 20 Bay Area congressional candidates in 1962 possessed many of the characteristics desired by voters. They were politically experienced, 13 having previously been elected to public office. The group was also well educated with the median candidate having completed 17 years of schooling, and with only one candidate not having attended college. The schools that the candidates attended were generally of high quality—14 of the 20 attended an Ivy League school, Stanford, or the University of California at some point in their educational career. The academic records of some of the candidates were available, and most candidates were better than average but not brilliant students.

Leadership experience and ability were possessed by many of the candidates. For example, all but a couple of "non-joiners" had held leadership positions in various community organizations and one third of the candidates had served as officers in the military service. (Another third had served as enlisted men.) Another kind of ability was indicated by the high incomes of most of the candidates; the estimated median income of about $19,000 was higher than that received by all but 5 percent of Bay Area families in 1959.

As was to be expected, not all of the candidates possessed all of the desired characteristics. Three of the candidates were divorced, with two of the three having remarried; one of these divorce and remarriage cases was well-remembered by a number of people in the area. A couple of the candidates were elderly, some had little previous public experience, and some were poor public speakers.

A comparison of the characteristics of incumbents and nonincumbents, Republicans and Democrats, sure winners, competitive candidates, and sure losers gives a much more complete and detailed picture of the characteristics of the candidates. Some of these comparisons are presented in Table 1. The leadership ability, administrative ability,

TABLE 1

Selected Personal Characteristics, Bay Area Congressional Candidates, 1962

Type of Candidate	Average Number of Years in Public Office	Average Number of Previous Campaigns[a]	Median Age	Median Years of Education	Median Dollar Income (estimated)	Percent Who Had Lived Less than 15 Years in California
Incumbents (8)	13	7	47	17	22,500[b]	13
Nonincumbents (12)	2	1	38	17	12,000	33
Republicans (10)	5	3	45	17	15–18,000	10
Democrats (10)	8	4	45	16	20–22,500	40
Sure winner (7)	13	7	48	19	22,500[b]	0
Competitive (6)	6	3	44	17	18–20,000	33
Sure loser (7)	1	[c]	33	16	10,000	43

Sources: Campaign materials and interviews with candidates.
[a]Campaigns for any public office.
[b]Congressional salary was $22,500, and some congressmen had other income.
[c]Less than 0.5.

speaking ability, and number of acquaintances of each of the candidates were also evaluated, based on observations and on the comments of campaign workers.

Incumbents were as a rule politically experienced and capable—men who had won their seats by defeating or scaring off the previous incumbent or by swamping their numerous opponents in the contest for a vacant seat. Few politically astute men cared to challenge such formidable foes; consequently the challenges were often made by relatively young and unskilled candidates. The open seats and the reapportioned seats in 1962 provided some hope, however, to the politically ambitious. As the table shows, incumbents had far more experience than nonincumbents, both as public officeholders and as campaigners. The average incomes of incumbents, bolstered by their $22,500 congressional salary, were also higher than those of nonincumbents. As a general rule, incumbents ranked higher than nonincumbents on the various measures of ability, and they had far more personal acquaintances in the district than nonincumbents, part of the reason being that a higher percentage of incumbents had lived in California for a long time. One advantage of nonincumbents was that of youth, but this advantage was relatively insignificant because only 2 of the 8 incumbents were over the normal retirement age of 65.

Differences between the parties were comparatively small, with candidates of each party being fairly similar on many measures. Democrats were a little more experienced than Republicans, and had slightly higher leadership abilities and incomes. Despite having averaged less time in California, they were judged to have more personal acquaintances than Republican candidates.

The characteristics of sure winners, competitive candidates, and sure losers provide some immediate evidence of why candidates ended up in these categories. Sure winners had more experience, income, leadership ability, speaking ability, administrative ability, and personal acquaintances than sure losers. Competitive candidates varied, usually ranking with the sure winners or falling midway between sure winners and sure losers. Many other indicators pointed

30 Becoming a Candidate

in the same direction. Sure winners and competitive candidates attended better schools than sure losers, stayed in school longer, and received higher grades while they were there. The occupations of the candidates indicated differences in ability, with sure winners and competitive candidates often being professional men, managers, or high level administrators, and sure losers engaging in such less prestigious occupations as stocks and bonds salesman, parttime accountant, newspaperman, and elementary school teacher.

Some indication of the importance of various characteristics is provided by an examination of the 9 nonincumbents who ran in districts that might have been competitive, comparing the 5 who ran a competitive or sure winning race with the 4 who were sure losers. The greatest differences between these two groups were in their political experience and income. The competitive candidates had served an average of almost 4 years in public office compared to none for the 4 sure losers. Similarly the 5 averaged one previous candidacy for office compared to no previous candidacies for the sure losers. The median competitive candidate had an estimated income of $18,000 compared to the $12,000 median for the sure losers. These findings suggest that competitive candidates are likely to come from the ranks of those who have run for office before and are interested in running again, or from the ranks of those with enough money and interest to provide some financing for a campaign. There were some less pronounced differences between the two groups in age, education, occupations, length of residence in California, and number of personal acquaintances, with competitive candidates being higher in each case. This discussion of experienced and inexperienced candidates and the comparison of nonincumbents who were able to make their races competitive with those who were not able to do so indicates the importance of experience. Not only is it the characteristic most desired by voters, but it is also important for the successful conduct of a campaign. Further aspects of the importance of experience will be presented in succeeding chapters, especially in the various comparisons of incumbents and nonincumbents.

SUMMARY

The acquisition of the campaign resource of candidacy involves problems of deciding to run and of deciding what personal qualities to emphasize in the campaign. The often-used classification of self-starters and recruits was not particularly useful for congressional races because most candidates could be classified as both. More useful was an analysis of the factors considered by prospective candidates before deciding to run, because it led to the finding that experienced candidates gave much more serious and accurate consideration to the potential effects that the campaign would have on their own lives. A comparison of the characteristics desired by voters and the characteristics of incumbents and nonincumbents showed that incumbents were more likely to have the personal characteristics that voters valued highly. An examination of the characteristics of nonincumbents who ran strong races with those who might have but did not revealed that the greatest differences between the two groups were in political experience and income, with the strong candidates being higher in each case. Differences between Republicans and Democrats were not particularly significant.

Chapter 3

ACQUIRING PARTY SUPPORT

Party loyalty provides an important base of voter support for most congressional candidates. Many voters comment that they always vote a straight ticket or support the party's candidates. Such votes are almost guaranteed to the winner of the primary election. Some of them may be lost, however, if party leaders withhold support, thus indicating that the candidate is not wholeheartedly the party's choice. As a result, a candidate's acquisition of party support requires not only winning a primary election but also winning the support of party leaders, who can in turn provide him with money, people, and other resources.

PRIMARY ELECTIONS

The acquisition and distribution of resources for primary elections may or may not be similar to the acquisition of resources for general elections—practically no studies are available exploring the similarities and differences. An important determinant would be the differences in attitudes of voters in primary elections as compared to voters in general elections. The usual assumption has been that the limited number of people who vote in primaries have attitudes different from those who vote in general elections, but a study in Wisconsin showed that voters in the 1966 gubernatorial primary held attitudes similar to nonvoters of the same party.[1] Even so, primary election voters cannot, for the most part, utilize the party label in making their decision, so that one or more other factors must necessarily be more significant in the primary than in the general election. In the 1964 SRC national survey, voters were asked for the most important reason for their vote in the congressional primary election. The first two reasons were coded in the same manner as were the general election responses reported at the beginning of Chapter 2. Among those who could remember the name of the candidate for whom they voted, the proportion of responses in each category was:[2]

	Percent
Candidate	64
Party	11
Issues	10
Group	2
Other	13
Total	100
Number of responses	(139)

A comparison with the general election findings reveals that the characteristics of the candidates were mentioned much more frequently in the primary, while issue and group responses were mentioned at approximately the same rate as in the general election. Surprisingly, even though the question was about primary elections, the responses of some voters fit into such coding categories as "Candidate's party affiliation. He is a (Democrat) (Republican)."

One well-substantiated difference between primary and general elections is that primaries are usually less com-

---

[1] Austin Ranney, "The Representativeness of Primary Electorates," paper delivered at the 1967 annual convention of the American Political Science Association. The view that primary election voters are unrepresentative of their party was presented by V. O. Key, Jr., *American State Politics: An Introduction,* Alfred A. Knopf, New York, 1956, pp. 145-152.
[2] Data from fall 1964 survey collected and tabulated by Survey Research Center, University of Michigan and made available by the Inter-university Consortium for Political Research.

petitive. As a result, candidates need fewer resources, on the average, in primary elections. One indication of less competition is that there are fewer contests in primary elections. In the 1960 congressional elections, there were competing candidates in more than 80 percent of the nation's districts in November, but in less than 40 percent of the primary elections.[3] Further evidence is provided by a comparison of victory margins. If 65 percent or more of the vote is regarded as constituting a lopsided win in a contested election, 70 percent of the incumbent congressmen who had primary election opponents had lopsided victories in the 1960 primary, but only 30 percent had lopsided victories over general election opponents.[4] Similar results are shown if competitiveness is measured by the defeat of incumbents. In the four congressional elections from 1954 through 1960 only about 1 percent of the nation's incumbent congressional candidates lost in the primary election, but about 6 percent lost in the general election.[5]

In the Bay Area in 1962, primary competition was much less significant than general election competition, only half of the candidates having competition in the primary. Even this proportion represented significantly more primary election competition than had been true in this area in previous years, with the 1961 redistricting probably being the cause of the difference.[6] Incumbents were much less likely to face a primary election challenge than were nonincumbents, and the two challenges that were made against incumbents were

[3] Compiled from data in Richard M. Scammon, ed., *America Votes 4: A Handbook of Contemporary American Election Statistics,* University of Pittsburgh Press, Pittsburgh, 1962.
[4] *Ibid.* Data on primary elections are from *Congressional Quarterly Almanac,* 16, 767 (1960).
[5] Compiled from data in *Congressional Quarterly Almanac:* 1954 edition, p. 719; 1956 edition, p. 760; 1958 edition, p. 722; and 1960 edition, pp. 766–767.
[6] John Voekel reported that there was a fairly steady increase in the amount of competition in primary elections in California from 1958 through 1964, but that nevertheless 1962 was an unusual year with more primary election competition than any of the other three elections. "An Analysis of the 1964 California Primary Election for State Legislative and Congressional Office," mimeographed manuscript at Institute of Governmental Studies, University of California, Berkeley, 1965.

weak, intended apparently to influence the incumbents rather than to defeat them.

Acquiring Campaign Resources[7]

The acquisition of campaign resources in the primary elections can be considered from the same approach as in the general election. The acquisition of candidacy would be no different. Because of the inadequacy of data, comparisons could not be made on the acquisition of issue information. In the acquisition, however, of party, group, financial, and worker resources, some important differences between primary and general elections were discovered.

The activity and intervention of party leaders were usually more limited in the primary election than in the general election. Such activity as was evident in the primary was by local leaders, with state and national leaders participating only in unusual circumstances. In the Republican party the local leaders who were active usually held official or semiofficial positions, but in the Democratic party the preprimary activists were usually leaders and members of the CDC clubs. Republican county central committees or semiofficial groups helped four of the six nonincumbent candidates, including two who had primary election opposition. The CDC clubs endorsed and supported candidates in most districts, but their poor record in the districts in which Democrats were likely to win new seats indicated that CDC endorsement was not essential to success. The endorsement process did serve, however, as an initial and relatively inexpensive test of political popularity.

Interest groups were less active before the primary than before the general election, the best evidence of the difference being the fact that they were more frequently listed as financial contributors in the general election. Labor unions, for example, contributed to at least 11 candidates in the general election but to only about 4 in the primary elec-

---

[7]Since field work was started too late to observe the primary election campaigns, the following comments, based on interviews and analyses of written reports and materials, are less accurate and less complete than are the comments on the general elections.

tion, although the total amount contributed was about the same in each election because they contributed very heavily to one unsuccessful primary campaign. Some other groups active in the primary elections included newspapers, which made endorsements, and peace and medical groups, each of which supported a favorite candidate.

Some distinct differences were found between the securing of finances in the primary and the general election campaigns. An analysis of campaign financial statements filed with the California Secretary of State showed that the amount of money raised in the primary was less than that in the general, the median reported by the 20 candidates being about $4400 in the primary and about $17,000 in the general election campaign. (These amounts exclude personal and family contributions.) Fewer people contributed to the primaries, at least twice as many contributing to the 20 general election candidates as contributed to the 32 primary candidates. Only 7 of the 20 candidates gave fairly complete listings of both primary and general election contributors but, judging by their reports, the average candidate could expect 13 times as many contributors in the general election as in the primary. This difference in the number of contributors in primary and general elections might be ascribed to the lowered competition of primary elections, which would allow candidates to get by with less money and thus fewer pleas to potential contributors. A more important factor, however, appears to be the public's lack of interest, a disinclination to contribute indicated by the relatively lower number of contributors even in the hotly contested primaries. The relative lack of public interest was also suggested by the fact that small contributors were more likely to contribute in the fall. For the 7 candidates mentioned above, contributions of $25 or less constituted 45 percent of the number of primary election contributions and 60 percent of the number of general election contributions.

Some variations were found in the sources of money for primary and general elections. Official and auxiliary party groups were more likely to contribute in general elections than in primary elections. They gave help to all 20 candidates in the general election, but to only half of them in the primary election. Primary election contributions were especially likely to go to unopposed Republicans or CDC-endorsed Democrats. On the other hand, candidates were slightly more likely to contribute personal, family, or borrowed funds to their primary election campaign than their general election campaign, and the total amount contributed by the 20 candidates and their families was slightly larger in the primary than in the general election campaign.

Variations were also found in the types of workers that candidates were able to recruit during the primary and general election campaigns. Respondents in the survey of campaign workers were asked what months they had worked for their congressional candidate. The total sample was divided into two groups, those who had worked in June or before (the primary election was June 5) and those who had not started campaign work until July or later. Most of the people in the first group also worked in the general election campaign, so that the variations between these two portions of the sample overstate the amount of variation between all primary and all general election workers. Our concern, however, is with the type of people who were mobilized in the spring versus the type mobilized in the fall. Primary election workers were more likely than general election workers to consider themselves personal friends of the candidate and to have worked for the candidate in previous campaigns. They were more likely to belong to political clubs and to identify strongly with their party. The intensity of party identification suggested that primary election workers might have had more extreme views than general election workers. This hypothesis was tested by comparing scores on a Role of the Federal Government scale; Democrats who worked in primary elections were found to be more liberal than Democrats who worked only in the general election, but there was no difference for Republicans.

In general, the differences in the Bay Area indicate that not only were primary elections less competitive than general elections, so that fewer resources were required, but that the level of public interest was much lower during the primary campaign, making it more difficult to mobilize resources. Only after campaigns had reached a high level in the autumn did the inexperienced workers, the small contributors, and the normally nonpolitical groups volunteer or even respond to the candidates' pleas for help. Consequently, candidates could rely less upon the resources that the public, parties, or groups could contribute, and had to rely more upon their own personal resources.

This greater reliance on personal resources in primary than in general elections helps to explain the comparatively greater advantage that incumbents have in primaries. Incumbents were much more likely than nonincumbents to possess the resources needed—personal knowledge about issues and personal friendships with party and group leaders, campaign workers, and financial contributors. In the general election campaign, many people became excited and active, and these people helped incumbents and nonincumbents alike; however, in the primary election, resources were comparatively scarce. Consequently, the candidates who possessed personal resources had distinct advantages.

SUPPORT OF PARTY LEADERS

Having won the party nomination, the candidate needs to acquire the support of the party leaders during the general election campaign. Because political parties (especially in California) have indefinite memberships and bureaucracies, the term "party leader" may have many different definitions. For purposes of this study, the definition used was that employed implicitly by the candidates: any person whose position, former position, or other characteristics indicated that he could influence voters in their capacity as party members, or influence the distribution of campaign resources possessed by or connected with the party. Generally this included those people holding formal positions with the party at the national, state, and local level, those party members holding public office, those people leading party auxiliary groups, and former holders of these positions. The support that party leaders could give candidates included endorsements, training, research, money, and workers. In the Bay Area, the principal means of securing the support of party leaders was by asking for it. Without such requests, party leaders, busy with the pressures of numerous campaigns, were likely to overlook a campaign, assuming that the candidate did not need or want support. The requests were usually for specific items—a letter of endorsement, extra money, or research assistance on a particular issue. Sure winners and competitive candidates were much more likely than sure losers to have their requests granted. Because sure winners did not need or request as much help, a large proportion of the resources went to the campaigns of competitive candidates. The most widely used indicator of the candidate's chances was the winner's vote percentage two years before; national party leaders generally designated as marginal the districts in which the winner received 50 to 55 percent of the vote in the last election. For those districts that had been changed by redistricting, the proportion of voters registered with each party provided an indication of chances for success. Polls and the candidate's record in previous elections also served as measures. One first-time Democratic candidate noted with chagrin that the proof he needed to convince party leaders evaporated on primary election day when he barely won despite the support of local party leaders and labor unions. In another district, party leaders withheld some financial contributions after taking a poll which showed that their candidate would probably lose.

Denials of support, especially by national level leaders, were not always explicit, and some candidates did not realize for some time that they had been "written off" as sure losers. One candidate came to this realization when his telephone calls to White House staff assistants suddenly stopped being returned. In another case a sure loser had the impression that his request for a national speaker for a fund-raising affair would be granted. Relying on this assumption, he borrowed a great deal of money, which he expected to repay from collections at the fund-raiser. National leaders wrote off the campaign but never bothered to notify the candidate that no speaker would be sent, so the borrowed money became the candidate's personal debt.

National Leaders

Whereas it was once believed that national officeholders should not participate in congressional elections, the President and Vice-President and prospective candidates for these offices have taken an increasingly active role in recent years. In 1954, 1958, and 1962 the men holding the offices of President and Vice-President engaged in strenuous attempts to influence congressional elections, their most conspicuous activity being speeches of endorsement in the congressional districts. In 1962, 17 Democratic and 3 Republican national party leaders, ranging from former presidents to national committee officials, came to the Bay Area to give speeches or hold press conferences at which they endorsed one or more congressional candidates. Endorsements by Democrats were not only more numerous but also more specific and more widely reported than endorsements by Republicans. Three more leaders, including President Kennedy, scheduled such speeches, but were forced to cancel them because of the Cuba crisis or the length of the congressional session. Sure winners and competitive candidates were more likely to receive endorsements than sure losers, a relationship indicated by the letters of endorsement sent by the President to various Democratic candidates. The only two nonincumbents to receive letters were competitive candidates John O'Connell and Robert Leggett. Sure losers said they tried hard, but were unable to get such letters. Apparently the President did not wish to be associated with hopeless campaigns, especially when the Republican incumbent might provide an occasional vote in Congress.

Each party has also regularly contributed assistance to congressional candidates through its national committee or its congressional campaign committee. The national committees have been more oriented toward the presidential campaigns and toward general and national issues, while the congressional campaign committees have been more concerned with congressional campaigns and the problems of particular districts and individual candidates.[8] In 1962 the committees provided money, speakers for fund-raising or interest-sparking affairs, research assistance, candidate schools, and campaign advice and assistance. The amounts of money contributed by national level committees ranged from nothing for some candidates to several thousand dollars for others. The differences depended largely upon competition, with competitive candidates averaging $2200 compared to $1000 for sure winners and $700 for sure losers. Republicans and Democrats received approximately equal amounts. The differences between incumbents and nonincumbents were also minor—$1300 to $1000—showing a distinct change for the national level committees from their original purpose of aiding the reelection of incumbents.[9] Research assistance varied widely but usually included materials criticizing the opposition, and for challengers, an analysis of the record of the incumbent they were challenging. Each national committee sponsored a training school in Washington, D.C., for its nonincumbent candidates, and the Republican Congressional Campaign Committee fieldman provided Republican candidates with advice on campaign techniques and procedures. Most of this nonmonetary assistance went to nonincumbents.

Official State and Local Leaders

The official political parties in California are notoriously weak and hamstrung by restrictive laws. However, this weakness should not be overstressed. California law does provide for official party congressional district campaign

[8]Hugh Bone, *Party Committees and National Politics*, University of Washington Press, Seattle, 1958, pp. 152, 153, 157. For an extended discussion of the role of national-level committees, see Charles L. Clapp, *The Congressman: His Work As He Sees It*, Brookings Institution, Washington, D.C., 1963, pp. 354–366. See also Floyd McCaffree and Arthur L. Peterson, "Training Programs of the Republican National Committee," *Journal of Social Issues*, 16, 30–39 (1960); Guy B. Hathorn, "Congressional and Senatorial Campaign Contributions in the Mid-term Election Year 1954," *Southwestern Social Science Quarterly*, 37, 207–221 (1956); and Cornelius P. Cotter and Bernard C. Hennessy, *Politics Without Power: The National Party Committees*, Atherton Press, New York, 1964.
[9]Bone, *op. cit.*, pp. 81, 156 had earlier reported such a change.

committees selected by the state central committee, and these committees are active in some districts. Many county central committees are also active. Official Republican party organizations have often established United Republican Finance Committees, which collect campaign funds for all party nominees.

In 1962, state party leaders gave little assistance beyond endorsements. Candidates in both parties felt that state leaders were so oriented toward the state campaigns that they had little time for the congressional campaigns. Relationships between congressional and statewide candidates seemed informal and casual, depending on personal situations rather than on widespread attempts to promote a party ticket. Some congressional candidates promoted party rallies, asking statewide candidates to come in, while others tried to avoid them. Democrats, especially Democratic challengers, emphasized these associations more than Republicans, but even these Democrats were likely to emphasize their association with President Kennedy more than their association with Governor Brown.

County central committees and congressional district campaign committees were active in some Bay Area districts, collecting money, sending out slate mailers, and establishing and maintaining precinct organizations. Most of the resources of some relatively inactive congressional candidacies were provided by county central committees, but many candidates who conducted active campaigns found themselves in sharp dispute with their county central committees. Some candidates felt that the central committees were siphoning off resources that should have been committed to the campaigns, while others found that the committees were so poorly organized that they were unable to provide the services needed for an active campaign, such as a precinct organization. Republican committees were generally more organized and active than Democratic committees, especially in the collection of funds. In fact, some nonincumbent Democratic candidates maintained that their county central committees discouraged activities that might have led to victory because the power structure on the committee would have been disturbed if a party candidate had been elected to public office. Incumbents were less dependent than nonincumbents on county central committees and were more familiar with their inadequacies. As a result, they were less embittered toward the committees at the end of the campaign. Association between congressional candidates and local candidates, especially candidates for the legislature, depended primarily upon the county central committee and the extent to which it could offer services to all candidates. If services, such as a precinct organization, fund raising, or a mailing to all party voters, were offered, they were usually accepted. In most cases such services were not offered, and each candidate went his own way.

Auxiliary Organization Leaders

In California many candidates have received support in recent years from the leaders of voluntary organizations, especially the California Republican Assembly and California Democratic Council. In 1962, Bay Area Democratic candidates received more support than did Republicans, indicated especially by the finding from the campaign worker survey that Democratic auxiliary groups contributed more workers than did Republican groups in 9 of the 10 districts. Bay Area Republican candidates generally agreed that the Federation of Republican Women was the largest and most active auxiliary group. Young Republicans gave significant assistance to some candidates and minor help to others. Various other Republican organizations, such as the California Republican Assembly, also provided minor assistance. California Democratic Council clubs provided the most support for Democratic candidates, contributing 4 times as many workers as the Young Democrats, the next most active organization, judged by responses to the campaign worker survey. Members of Democratic auxiliary groups gave more support to nonincumbents than to incumbents, while members of Republican groups gave more support to incumbents. The explanation apparently is that there are simply more auxiliary group members in the middle-class and suburban districts in which Republicans are regularly the incumbents and Democrats the challengers than there are in other districts. Certainly in the case of the CDC, membership figures in June 1963 showed that there were more CDC members in most of the Bay Area districts then represented by a Republican than in most of the districts then represented by a Democrat.[10]

Party Splits

In some districts the healing of local party splits was especially important in securing support. (In some of the Eastern and Midwestern states, factional disputes may be more bitterly contested, but the losers are apparently not as likely to decide to support the opposite party.) The CDC split in the primary in one district, with some clubs withdrawing support from the endorsed candidate in favor of the eventual winner. Leaders of the secessionist movement resigned after the primary in an effort to reduce acrimony and increase party support for the candidate. In the Fourth District, Democratic nominee Robert Leggett attempted to overcome the effects of a divisive primary by frequent publication of pictures showing him and his primary opponent in friendly poses. In California, there seemed to be no special technique for healing such splits except to plead for party loyalty or, if this were not successful, to attempt to isolate the primary election loser and thus to indicate that he represented only a small faction.

Such splits occasionally provided an opportunity for opponents, and they serve as illustration of the fact that in the Bay Area a fairly highly developed technique was that of denying the opponent the support of his own party or, at least of neutralizing that support. Such denials or neutralizations were accomplished by securing endorsements from the leaders of the opposite party or by forming clubs of supporters from that party.

The most extensive of these activities were in the Sixth District, where Republican Congressman William Mailliard undermined the Democratic party support of John

[10] Leonard Rowe, *Preprimary Endorsements in California Politics*, Bureau of Public Administration, University of California, Berkeley, 1961, pp. 37, 51–54 has reported similar statistics on a statewide level.

O'Connell. Mailliard's principal tactic was that of securing public support from prominent Democrats, some of whom appreciated Mailliard's support of shipping interests, and most of whom admired Mailliard's moderation and feared O'Connell's "radicalism," as they expressed it. Mailliard asked for and received the early endorsement of three prominent Democrats, a former vice-chairman of the Democratic National Committee, a former treasurer of the Committee, and a labor union official. (Two of the three were associated with the shipping industry.) These three served as vice-chairmen of a Mailliard campaign committee and signed a letter to all Democratic voters in the district, which stated:

> Our Committee loyally supports President Kennedy, Governor Brown and all but one of our party's candidates. That exception is John A. O'Connell, Mailliard's opponent. Here we cross party lines and vigorously oppose O'Connell *on his record*.

Other Democratic supporters won by Mailliard included two of his former opponents and the wife of another former opponent. The immediate past chairman of the San Francisco County Democratic Central Committee, who had been O'Connell's primary election opponent, publicly endorsed Mailliard. These endorsements were apparently secured as a result of personal requests by Mailliard, who said that a significant portion of his campaign time was devoted to securing this support. In fact, Mailliard stated that he had lined up the support of 20 more prominent Democrats but that Democratic Governor Edmund (Pat) Brown, fearing large scale Democratic defections, had pressured these people into remaining silent. Mailliard also received (and used) letters of commendation from Secretary of State Dean Rusk and Democratic Congressman Herbert Bonner, chairman of the Merchant Marine and Fisheries Committee on which Mailliard served. O'Connell attempted to counteract Mailliard's activities by placing strong emphasis on the support that he had from party leaders and, specifically, from elected officials such as President Kennedy and Governor Brown.

At least one fourth of the candidates established opposite party or citizens clubs. For example, the Citizens for Leggett group was composed of Republicans and Independents who were supporting Democratic candidate Leggett. These clubs were largely paper organizations, set up to legitimize a mailing or to exploit one or two well-known names. Nevertheless, support from the opposite party was often genuine, and the survey of campaign workers showed that at least half of the candidates had workers who considered themselves members of the opposite party. For these candidates, opposite-party workers comprised 5 to 15 percent of all of their campaign workers.

SUMMARY

The acquisition of the party resource depended partially on success in the primary election. Because public interest in politics is much lower for primary than for general elections, campaign resources are much more difficult to secure in the primary. As a result, incumbents, who possess significant personal resources, have distinctly greater advantages over the challengers in primaries than they have over the challengers in general elections. The party resource also involves the support of party leaders, especially national and local leaders. Large proportions of the resources that party leaders controlled, such as money, training, research assistance, and workers, were channeled into competitive campaigns. Sure winners did not need nor request such help, and the requests of sure losers were not granted (thus helping to insure that they would lose). The principal differences between the parties were based on party structure, with Republicans receiving comparatively more help from official local party organizations, and Democrats receiving more from auxiliary groups, just as they had in the primary election campaigns. A surprising similarity was the requests of candidates in both parties for public endorsements from Democratic party leaders, but this action by Republicans is understandable in view of the fact that voters registered as Democrats outnumbered those registered as Republicans in every district, in many cases by a three-to-two margin. (The success of the Republican candidates indicates that many of these people vote Republican despite their registration.) Because incumbents were party leaders themselves, they were less likely to need party support, and they were less likely to request it. Despite their acknowledged party leadership, incumbents had much greater success than nonincumbents in securing the support of leaders of the opposite party.

Chapter 4

ACQUIRING ISSUE INFORMATION

When asked the most important reason for their vote decisions in congressional races, voters have mentioned attitudes toward issues less frequently than attitudes toward candidates and parties. Nevertheless, enough people have mentioned issues to indicate some importance, especially in close races. Furthermore, issue positions may have some distinct significance in the acquisition of other resources, such as money, workers, and group support.

The acquisition of the issue resource involves much more than just taking a stand, because candidates do not necessarily win votes by airing their prejudices. To be effective a candidate should emphasize issues that are considered significant by his constituency and on which his view is supported by a substantial segment of the constituency. Selecting these issues requires information on voter opinions; defending one's views about them requires information on their content.

DETERMINING VOTER OPINIONS

Voter opinions about issues can be determined from several sources. Two studies, one in the 1940's and one in the 1960's, reported the results of asking Congressmen to rate several sources for their usefulness in determining public attitudes. Each study found personal contact and mail to be important, followed by newspapers and opinion polls.[1]

Mail

Other studies have indicated that the picture of public opinion presented by the mail may well be distorted. Some of the mail is inspired by pressure groups although this type of mail is apparently easily spotted and given its proper weight.[2] Most of the mail a congressman receives comes from only about 15 percent of the adult population. The writers of letters are better educated than the general population, hold higher status occupations, and are more likely to have an immediate economic stake in the government. As a result of these differences between letter writers and the general population, the mail to Congress on some occasions strongly favored one position, while public opinion polls indicated a different attitude. On other occasions, little or no mail was received on vital issues.[3] The mail may also give an individual congressman a biased view of public attitudes because people are more likely to write to officials with whom they agree than to officials with whom they disagree. Despite these limitations, the mail has value because it gives some indication of the issues important to a portion of the public, of the views of this portion, and of the intensity of their views. Finally, because letters come from supporters more than from opponents, the mail can give a congressman some idea of the views of the people who are most likely to work for his reelection.[4] The average congressman receives over 100 letters

[1] Martin Kriesberg, "What Congressmen and Administrators Think of the Polls," *Public Opinion Quarterly*, 9, 334 (1945); John H. Kessel, "The Washington Congressional Delegation," *Midwest Journal of Political Science*, 8, 4, 7 (1964).
[2] Robert E. Lane, *Political Life: Why People Get Involved in Politics*, The Free Press, Glencoe, Illinois, 1959, pp. 67–74.
[3] Rowena Wyant, "Voting Via the Senate Mailbag," *Public Opinion Quarterly*, 5, 372–374 (1941). See also Philip M. DeVany, "The 'Town Meeting' Poll in South Dakota," *Public Opinion Quarterly*, 18, 138 (1954).
[4] This is especially true of mail but use of most sources of information about constituent opinion will give a more accurate picture of the views of supporters than of opponents. Kessel, *op. cit.*, p. 7.

every day, so he has a large sample of opinion.[5]

In the Bay Area, mail appeared to be more valuable for congressmen than for nonincumbents as a source of information about voter attitudes. As an example, Bay Area congressmen received, during the 1965 session, many letters about a Federal Communications Commission proposal to limit the broadcasting power of FM radio stations, letters stimulated by the numerous FM stations in the area. Consequently, most, if not all Bay Area congressmen were prepared to discuss the FCC ruling and the prospects for its enforcement, but no nonincumbent indicated even an awareness of this subject as an issue. This example suggests that one of the values of mail is its indication of the issues that are personally significant to constituents, even though they may not be of national significance. Only one nonincumbent mentioned the receipt of mail, and the letters he received were about the incumbent's stand on an issue.

There appeared to be no correlations between mail as a source of information and party or competitiveness, except that the aide to one Republican, in explaining his incumbent's failure to maintain a year-round district office, stated that constituents in his district were accustomed to writing letters and were able to solve their problems without personal interviews. Constituents in the neighboring Democratic district, according to this aide, needed a local congressional office because of their relative inability to express themselves in correspondence. To the extent that this thesis is true, representatives of populations with a high educational level (usually Republican) would receive more mail than representatives of populations with a low educational level (usually Democratic). Data were not available to test the thesis.

Personal Contact

The Bay Area candidates engaged in varying amounts of personal contact, ranging from one candidate who did no

[5] U.S. Congress, House of Representatives, Committee on Appropriations, Subcommittee on Legislative Branch Appropriations, Ninetieth Congress, First Session, *Hearings on Legislative Branch Appropriations for 1968*, U.S. Government Printing Office, Washington, D.C., 1967, p. 277.

Determining Voter Opinions 51

more than ring a few doorbells, attend some parties, and make a half dozen speeches, to another candidate who campaigned steadily for a year and a half and met 100 or more people on each of the days that he was observed campaigning. Most candidates seemed to sense voter attitudes from these contacts. One Republican congressman, discussing what he had learned from the campaign, said: "I knew people were concerned about medicare but I didn't realize they were *that* concerned." Some neophytes reported that they were surprised to learn that the average voter had little interest in politics.

Incumbents had several significant advantages in their personal contacts. They regularly received visits from constituents and lobbyists in Washington. During the campaign, their time for personal contacts was limited by the length of the congressional session, but the contacts they did make were more fruitful than the contacts nonincumbents made. When incumbents spoke to a group, people often responded by murmuring agreement, uttering gasps of surprise, and asking questions that expressed their views about issues, even though the congressmen may not have mentioned any issues in their talks. In contrast, there was rarely any audience response during the talk of a nonincumbent, and there were usually only a few questions. The questions would relate to the campaign or to congressional procedures rather than to issues, even though the candidate may have spent his whole speech on issues. Incumbents also appeared to be able to see more people in a given period of time than nonincumbents, one reason being that the incumbents usually drew larger crowds. The availability of an incumbent's district office with a permanent address, a listed telephone, and a trained staff increased opportunities for personal contacts because these factors often made it easier for a constituent to arrange a meeting with a congressman than with his opponent.

Polls

Public opinion polls available to congressmen or congressional candidates are of two types: (1) professional polls that are purchased from commercial polling agencies, and (2) congressional polls that are conducted by mailing questionnaires from the congressman's office to a large sample of constituents. Louis Harris estimated that professional polls were used by one tenth of all congressional candidates in 1962.[6] In the Bay Area, they were used by about 6 of the 20 candidates.[7] Although polls are usually considered top-secret, copies or descriptions of the 4 best ones were made available by campaign personnel. Generally the polls were of the type described as "quick and dirty." One poll was conducted by mailing double post cards to potential respondents, asking them to indicate their choice between candidates and to return the card. The procedure is essentially the same as that used by the *Literary Digest* in 1936 when it predicted a landslide for Alf Landon over Franklin Roosevelt. The *Digest* was laughed out of business, and few, if any, reputable pollsters have used such techniques since then. Another poll used telephone interviews. Not surprisingly, the pollster's report indicated that two thirds of the voters were women (husbands were gone during the day while the calls were made), and most people were financially comfortable, at least rich enough to own a telephone. (There were no telephones in about one sixth of the homes in that district, and these were mostly poorer homes.) Only one pollster used trained,

[6] Louis Harris, "Polls and Politics in the United States," *Public Opinion Quarterly*, **27**, 3 (1963). One of the first uses of a professional poll by a congressional candidate was by Jacob Javits in 1946. Jacob Javits, "How I Used a Poll in Campaigning for Congress," *Public Opinion Quarterly*, **11**, 222–226 (1947).
[7] The reason for the approximation is that it was not always clear that a poll, and not a voter registration drive, was purchased. The determination of the proportion of candidates using polls requires a definition of the number of candidates and of the professionalism needed to make a poll professional. Should the number of candidates include only the major party nominees, as was done above, or should the defeated primary election candidates who hired pollsters be added to the list? How should one count prospective candidates, such as the Bay Area man who decided not to run for Congress after seeing the results of a poll he ordered? Is a poll professional if it is conducted by postcard or by volunteers telephoning? For this study, a poll was considered professional if someone was hired and paid to conduct it, a definition which is quite inclusive.

experienced interviewers. Sample size was usually about 400, adequate for the pollster's purposes, but samples often excluded rural areas and out-of-the-way places. For his money—$500 to $3000—the candidate usually received a brief report giving the percentages of responses for each choice in some of the questions and, occasionally, a breakdown of the preferences of various demographic groups. Only one report listed the actual questions asked, and no candidate received IBM cards or interview protocols that he might have used for further analysis of his own. Due to inadequacies of the original questions, only one pollster was able to tell the candidate what issues were considered important by the voters. Judged by their reports, pollsters saw their role as that of campaign strategist and tactician, and they presented numerous suggestions. Candidates were urged, for example, to use larger bumper strips, to appear at Catholic functions, and to call for more education on Communism—suggestions which often had little to do with the results of the polls.

Campaign managers were more likely to receive and use the polls than candidates, one reason being that candidates might become discouraged by the results. In one case, in which the pollster gave the poll to the candidate against the manager's wishes, the figures in black and white, although they had been expected at that stage of the campaign, so disheartened the candidate that the campaign was slowed for about two weeks. Generally the polls were used as one of the determinants for planning campaign strategy. One poll was taken in early spring[8] and showed the candidate to be leading. Based on this information, a successful "don't rock the boat" campaign was planned and conducted. Despite their use of polls, some managers stoutly asserted that they had only limited confidence in them, which was just as well, given the unrepresentative samples, poorly trained interviewers, and inadequate analyses. (Of course, if candidates or managers had been more familiar with polling procedures, they would

[8]The results of the poll were released publicly just before the November election, phrased in a manner to indicate that the poll had been taken very recently.

have had a better basis for knowing which of the findings, if any, were reliable.) Professional polls were used almost exclusively in competitive races although they might well have been useful to some sure losers who, if they had polled, might have realized that they had no chance and could have saved their campaign money. High costs of the polls kept several candidates from using them. There was apparently little or no difference between Republicans and Democrats or between incumbents and nonincumbents.

Congressional polls are more widely used. The polls have often been used as campaign devices—voters are flattered that the congressmen should ask their opinion—and, as a result, congressmen have often been relatively unconcerned with the accuracy of the sample, the bias of the question, the rate of return, or the direction of the response. (Congressional polls suffer from many of the same problems as postcard polls and mail, in that the original samples are not likely to be representative of the population, and the people who return mail questionnaires differ from the population, usually being better educated and more interested in the subject of the questionnaire.) In the late 1950's, some congressmen became increasingly interested in using congressional polls as a means of sampling opinion in their districts, and they stressed the use of more professional procedures. The proportion of congressmen who use congressional polls has increased from 11 percent in 1954 to between 27 and 50 percent in 1963–1964. The technique has been adopted especially by younger congressmen.[9]

Six of the Bay Area congressmen—all but the 2 Democrats with the safest seats—conducted congressional polls in 1962 or before. Generally the questionnaires were sent to every family or registered voter, or to every householder and RFD boxholder. The paper and printing costs of about $1000 were usually borne by the congressman or his last campaign

[9]Walter Wilcox, "The Congressional Poll—and Non-Poll," *Political Opinion and Electoral Behavior: Essays and Studies*, edited by Edward C. Dreyer and Walter A. Rosenbaum, Wadsworth Publishing Company, Belmont, California, 1966, pp. 390–391, 400.

treasury, and the addressing was often done by party workers in the district. The letters were mailed under the congressman's frank, and the respondent furnished the envelope and postage for the reply. Usually 10 to 20 questions were asked about issues then before Congress. Respondents were commonly given a choice of "yes," "no," or "undecided," and were encouraged to submit additional comments. The selection of subjects and the wording of questions often reflected the attitudes of the congressmen. For example, in 1964, 2 of the congressmen asked questions on the proposed congressional pay raise then before Congress. One asked:

> A bill is now pending before Congress which would increase the salary of members of Congress from $22,500 per year to $32,500 per year. Would you favor this 44% increase in congressional salaries?

The question of the other Congressman was:

> Do you approve the recommendation of a Presidential Commission to raise congressional salaries to $32,500?

Not surprisingly, in view of the emphasis on a 44 percent increase as compared to the emphasis on a presidential commission, the first congressman found his district less favorable to the pay raise and voted against it, while the second found his district more favorable and voted for it.

Response rates were good for a mass mailing, ranging from 10 to 20 percent, for a total of 20,000 to 35,000 replies. The replies were tabulated by the congressman's office staff or by volunteers. The congressmen felt that the polls often gave them a good interpretation of constituent opinion. One congressman, who personally read all of the comments added to the questionnaires, stated that he felt a greater sense of communication with his constituency then than at any other time.

SEARCH FOR INFORMATION ON ISSUES

Very little scholarly material has been published on the candidate's search for information on the content of issues

Acquiring Issue Information

— information, for example, about the specific proposals in bills before Congress and the arguments advanced for and against these proposals. One reason for this may be that such a search may not have been significant in political campaigns in previous years. If so, political debates between candidates and the increased sophistication of the public required such a search by many candidates in 1962. Another reason may be that scholars have been unaware of the searches which were conducted by candidates. Certainly in this Bay Area study, the importance and magnitude of such searches had not been anticipated, and were realized only after observing several presumably well-informed candidates working hard on this task. Today's congressional candidate needs to prepare extensively on issues—not only on issues he considers important, but also on issues his opponent may raise in a debate, and on issues that voters may ask about.

Of the 3 factors of incumbency, party, and competitiveness, the first is the most significant in the search for information, so significant, in fact, that it is fruitless to discuss patterns without first classifying the candidates into incumbents and nonincumbents. The 8 Bay Area incumbents had served 4 to 18 years in Congress, discussing issues with colleagues, attending committee hearings, and listening to debates; consequently they were well informed on the policy content of issues. During the campaign, each congressman also had at least 1 administrative assistant in his district who could do research if need be, and most (if not all) of the congressmen brought home 2 or 3 steamer trunks filled with such materials as their voting records and information on bills which had been before Congress. If these were not sufficient, each congressman had immediate and official access to the Library of Congress, which includes the Legislative Reference Service. (The average congressman makes more than 325 requests for information each year from the Library of Congress.)[10] Given these resources, incumbents spent little of their campaign time gathering information about the content of issues.

This was not so with nonincumbents. The average nonin-

[10]Compiled from figures in Charles Clapp, *The Congressman: His Work as He Sees It,* Brookings Institution, Washington, D.C., 1963, p. 113.

cumbent was forced to give up part of his campaign time to gather information, and the choice of how much time to give up was always hard. One nonincumbent decided to rely on the information he already had. As a result, when he appeared before a group of teen-agers from his own party, he was forced into several embarrassing admissions of unfamiliarity with the issues they raised. Admittedly some of the issues were esoteric, such as the advisability of the United States' support for royalists in Yemen; nevertheless, the audience was left with the impression that the candidate was poorly informed. A second nonincumbent decided to concentrate on the issues. His campaign workers became discouraged at the limited amount of time he had left for campaigning but the candidate maintained that he would recoup in a series of debates scheduled with the incumbent. The candidate did reasonably well in the debates, but the crowds were disappointingly small. On the one occasion when the challenger asked if there was anyone in the audience who had not already decided how to vote, only a teen-age girl in the front row raised her hand.

For the nonincumbents who decided to gather information, a number of sources were available in addition to the books, newspapers, and magazines with which the candidates were already familiar. The national-level committees of each party provided candidates with material in a number of different forms. The committees sent much printed material by mail, but most candidates did not have time to read it during the campaign. (In contrast, incumbents had been receiving this material during the off-campaign periods and consequently had had more time to read and digest it.) The committees also provided candidates with some information especially relevant to their campaigns. For example, the Democratic Congressional Campaign Committee provided each of its candidates running against a Republican incumbent with information on the number of bills the incumbent had introduced and the percentage that had been passed by Congress.[11] Training schools conducted in Washington, D.C.

[11] In one case the information was inaccurate, to the dismay of the Democratic candidate who was forced to admit his error during a televised debate.

were especially valuable for the nine candidates who attended. Programs at these schools included discussions of such topics as foreign policy, taxes, trade, social security, and education.

Another source of information frequently used by nonincumbents was local people who were well informed. Requests for information were often made to local public officials and government employees, especially by candidates who held local office. Some Bay Area candidates relied on their campaign workers for issue information. Three candidates established issue advisory committees with varying results. In one case the committee, made up of political activists and politically oriented professors, gradually became the steering committee for the whole campaign. In another case the candidate formed a committee of 20 college professors, apparently men with limited political experience. The candidate's disillusionment with his committee was illustrated by his casting aside of a partially read technical report on the gold outflow with the phrase "I read the papers too." Such a result from an issue advisory committee is not particularly surprising. Previous studies have noted that the committees have limited usefulness because candidates tend to rely more upon their campaign staffs than upon issue committees as the campaign progresses. The members of the committees are usually neither physically close enough to the campaign nor familiar enough with the political and practical aspects of the subject to satisfy the needs of the candidates in the way that an experienced staff can.[12]

Democrats conducted a more active search for information about the content of issues than did Republicans, considering nonincumbents only, for no differences could be detected among incumbents. Democratic nonincumbents tried such techniques as establishing issue advisory committees, subscribing to *Congressional Quarterly Weekly Report* and the *Congressional Record*, and hiring a Washington, D.C., re-

[12]For one such example, see Bryant Danner, *Campaign Decision-makers*, City Politics Report, Boston Related Document No. 4, series edited by Edward C. Banfield; Joint Center for Urban Studies of the Massachusetts Institute of Technology and Harvard University, Cambridge, 1960, Chapter 4.

search agency, but there was no evidence of such efforts by Republican nonincumbents. All of the Democratic nonincumbents attended their National Committee's training program in Washington, D.C., while only three of the six Republicans attended. Competitiveness seemed less significant as a variable than party or incumbency. The only relationship found was that, among nonincumbents, competitive candidates were slightly more likely than sure losers to attend training schools and conduct active searches for information about the policy content of issues.

SUMMARY

The acquisition of issue information requires that candidates learn about public attitudes toward issues and about the substantive content of the issues. The tasks are time consuming and expensive, but failure to undertake them may lead to embarrassment and loss of votes. Incumbents had significant advantages in both tasks. They found it easier to determine constituency opinion because they received more mail, because their personal contacts with constituents were more fruitful, and because they could use their franking privilege to poll large numbers of voters in their district at low cost. Incumbents entered the campaigns with practically all of the information they needed about the policy content of issues. If they did need to search for more information, numerous sources were easily available. In contrast nonincumbents received little mail, they found it difficult to get people to talk about issues, and they found the cost of professional polls often beyond their resources. Nonincumbents were less informed than incumbents, and they could ill afford to spend campaign time becoming informed. The sources available to nonincumbents were usually poorer than those available to incumbents, consisting, for example, of campaign workers instead of the Legislative Reference Service. Differences between parties appeared to be minor, Democratic nonincumbents showing more interest than Republican nonincumbents in learning the content of issues, and Republican incumbents being more likely than Democratic incumbents to conduct congressional polls. (The latter finding is true on the national level also.)[13] The characteristics of their constituencies indicate that Democratic congressmen may receive more personal visits from constituents, while Republicans receive more mail. The differences on mail would be relevant to responses on congressional polls, because it indicates that Republican congressmen would receive a higher response from their polls. Therefore they would be more satisfied and more likely to continue to use them. Differences based on competitiveness indicated that candidates in competitive districts were more likely than candidates in non-competitive districts to search for issue information, especially information about public attitudes. Competitive candidates had more personal contact than noncompetitive candidates, and they were more likely to hire professional polls and conduct congressional polls. If candidates in competitive districts searched more than candidates in noncompetitive districts for information on voter opinions, then presumably they were more accurately informed about voter attitudes, and possibly their congressional votes and actions, assuming electoral success, were more representative of voter views than the votes and actions of elected candidates from noncompetitive districts.[14]

---

[13]Wilcox, *op. cit.*, p. 399.
[14]The causal factors may be age and experience rather than competitiveness. The importance of age is indicated by the finding that younger congressmen are more likely to conduct congressional polls, and by Lewis Dexter's report that younger congressmen pay more attention to their mail than do older congressmen. Lewis Dexter, "What Do Congressmen Hear: The Mail," *Public Opinion Quarterly*, **20**, 17 (1956). A possible explanation for the effect of age is presented in Chapter 9 where it is noted that experienced candidates (who presumably are older) were more likely to believe in the Burkean theory of representation, while inexperienced candidates were more likely to believe that a congressman should vote as his district wished. Thus the inexperienced candidates would presumably make greater efforts to learn the views of their districts. Age and experience would be related to competitiveness to the extent that the greater turnover in competitive districts resulted in younger congressmen from those districts.

Chapter 5

ACQUIRING THE SUPPORT OF NONPARTY GROUPS

The electoral decisions of some voters are affected by groups—groups to which they belong or groups that they identify with or against. (Some voters will oppose a candidate, for example, because he is supported by labor unions, to which they are opposed.) In national surveys, only about 3 percent of the respondents have mentioned that they voted for a congressional candidate because they believed he or his opponent would or would not do something for some group. Analyses have indicated, however, that the votes of 10 percent or more of the members of a group may be affected by decisions of the group leadership to support or oppose a candidate. Even if the leadership does not take a position, a similar proportion of members may be affected by the fact that one candidate is a member of the group, as, for example, when Catholics vote more strongly for a Catholic candidate than they would have for a non-Catholic.[1] Such group-influenced votes may be very important in some congressional races. In addition, groups can provide many of the resources needed in a campaign—workers, money, audiences, access to mass media, access to community leaders, and access to other groups.

[1] Angus Campbell, Philip E. Converse, Warren E. Miller, and Donald E. Stokes, *The American Voter*, John Wiley and Sons, New York, 1960, pp. 314–321.

VALUE OF PARTICULAR GROUPS

From which groups should candidates request support? If the time and energy required are to be spent fruitfully, requests should usually be restricted to groups that have some interest in politics, to groups that are large enough to have sufficient resources so that their support will be meaningful, and to groups that have substantial prestige, if the support is to be announced publicly. The type of support a candidate can expect from a group will depend upon the resources the group possesses, such as people, money, influence, or intellect, and on the legitimacy of the group. Groups whose participation is not considered legitimate, such as liquor dealers in some areas, will probably contribute those resources that can be given covertly, such as money.

Groups vary widely in the amount of interest they have in politics. Some groups that are organized for political purposes, such as the Americans for Democratic Action, the Americans for Constitutional Action, and the Committee on Political Education (AFL-CIO), have a very high interest. Among groups organized for nonpolitical purposes, the amount of political interest usually depends upon the extent to which governmental action can or does affect the interests of the group, and the extent to which group members and the public feel that it is proper for the group to participate in politics.

Many of the groups that have participated extensively in politics in the post-World War II period can be placed in one of the categories below.[2]

1. Business groups,[3] especially the following ones.

    (a) Those who sell services to the government (such as contractors).

[2]Some indication of the types of groups that have a continuing political interest is provided by checking reports of lobby expenditures before Congress. Some groups, such as the National Association of Manufacturers, do not file reports so that the list is not necessarily complete. See the annual issues of the *Congressional Quarterly Almanac* for such listings.
[3]Just as the California Democratic Council and the California Republican Assembly were formed after their parties had lost control of the national government, businessmen, after being badly defeated in the 1958 elections,

(b) Those concerned with taxation provisions (such as the petroleum industry and the savings and loan industry).
(c) Those regulated by the government (such as utilities and liquor).

2. Labor unions, especially the United Auto Workers of America, the United Steel Workers of America, the International Ladies Garment Workers Union, the International Association of Machinists, and the Teamsters Union.[4]

3. Groups of government employees such as the National Federation of Postal Clerks and the National Education Association.

4. Medical and health groups, such as the American Medical Association.

5. Veterans groups, such as the American Legion and the Veterans of Foreign Wars.

6. Farm groups, such as the Farm Bureau or the Farmers Union.

The public's awareness of and attitudes toward various groups have been measured in some public opinion polls. Potentially the most effective groups, judged by the results, are Protestant church groups, veterans organizations, some business groups such as the Chamber of Commerce, some professional groups such as the American Medical Association, and some farm organizations such as the Farm Bureau. Most labor unions have a balanced effect on the general public with about equal proportions of the population being more willing and less willing to support a candidate because of union endorsement. The business and veterans organizations gain their strength from their influence on the general public, since they have comparatively small memberships. Church and labor groups have less positive influence on the

began to encourage each other to become active in politics. Some companies established political training programs for management employees. For reports and evaluations of this movement, see Andrew Hacker and Joel D. Aberbach, "Businessmen in Politics," *Law and Contemporary Problems*, **27**, 266–279 (1962); and "Businessmen Getting into Practical Politics," *Congressional Quarterly Weekly Report* (April 3, 1959), pp. 490–491.

[4] Nicholas Masters, "The Organized Labor Bureaucracy as a Base of Support for the Democratic Party," *Law and Contemporary Problems*, **27**, 253 (1962).

general public, but they do have positive influence on their large memberships. Open support of a candidate by some unpopular organizations such as the John Birch Society or the Teamsters Union is clearly harmful, judged by the reactions of the general public. Many other groups are not well enough known to have a large effect upon the national electorate. For example, such political groups as the Committee on Political Education (AFL-CIO), Americans for Constitutional Action, Americans for Democratic Action, and American Civil Liberties Union have been "heard of" by only a minority of the national population, often less than one third.[5]

In individual constituencies particular groups may be more or less prestigious and more or less willing to participate in politics. One group that has participated extensively in California politics is newspapers, which commonly endorse candidates in both primary and general elections. One survey of politically informed people around the state found that local newspapers were rated as the most influential group in local elections. Newspapers were especially significant in the large cities while merchants, service clubs, and lay church groups were more important in the small towns.[6]

[5] Howard E. Freeman and Morris Showel, "Differential Political Influence of Voluntary Associations," *Public Opinion Quarterly*, 15, 707 (1952); *The New York Times*, July 31, 1964 (story reporting a poll conducted by Opinion Research Corporation of Princeton, N.J.); Hadley Cantril, ed., *Public Opinion 1935–1946*, Princeton University Press, Princeton, 1951, pp. 569, 635; Bernard R. Berelson, Paul F. Lazarsfeld, and William N. McPhee, *Voting: A Study of Opinion Formation in a Presidential Campaign*, University of Chicago Press, Chicago, 1954, p. 168 (footnote 2); David C. Leege, "1964 Election Survey – Boone County, Missouri," *University of Missouri Business and Government Review*, 7, 39 (March-April 1965). See also the 1960 national survey available through the Inter-university Consortium for Political Research, which has similar findings, plus data indicating distrust of minority – Negro, Jewish, Catholic – groups. Some of the polls asked voters if they would be likely to take advice from or trust particular groups, and others asked if the support of a group for a candidate would make the voter more or less likely to vote for the candidate.

[6] Eugene C. Lee, *The Politics of Nonpartisanship: A Study of California City Elections*, University of California Press, Berkeley, 1960, pp. 76–90. For other comments on the importance of newspaper endorsements, see Charles Clapp, *The Congressman: His World as He Sees It*, Brookings Institution, Washington, D.C., 1963, p. 390; and Reo M. Christenson, "The Power of the Press: The Case of *The Toledo Blade*," *Midwest Journal of Political Science*, 3, 227–240 (1959).

Willingness of groups to participate in politics also depends upon the political culture of various areas. In the city of San Francisco all sorts of groups—social, civic, business, and political—are accustomed to endorsing candidates after hearing them or their representatives in public meeting. In other areas nonparty groups are less highly organized, less politicized, and less willing to endorse or help candidates. One campaign manager went so far as to complain that nobody in his district belonged to anything, and no group was interested in either of the candidates.

TECHNIQUES FOR SECURING GROUP SUPPORT

The principal techniques for securing group support can be categorized as follows.
 1. Presenting a suitable record on public issues. Some groups compile voting records, thus appearing to endorse those congressmen who voted for the group's objectives most frequently.
 2. Requesting endorsements or help from representatives of the group or from prominent individuals in the group.
 3. Requesting official endorsements, which are given most regularly by the political action committees of labor unions.
 4. Making appeals to the group membership by means of speeches, letters, or advertisements. Sometimes such appeals are made by the formation of a "Veterans for Jones" type group, the usual purpose being to legitimize some mailings or press releases.
 5. Purchasing endorsements.

The fifth technique was practiced only in the city of San Francisco. Candidates and campaign managers in that city reported that the economic viability of some of the ethnic newspapers depended upon the purchase of advertisements (and endorsements) by political candidates. One San Francisco candidate also said that he was given the opportunity to purchase for $7.50 the right to make a speech to members of a group, but he declined. Some San Francisco groups allowed any person who had paid his $1 membership fee to vote on the group's endorsements, and some candidates reportedly urged their friends to pay the fee and vote in the endorsing session. Only the first category does not involve active solicitation by the candidates, who usually find themselves trying to stimulate groups to become involved in politics. Most nonpolitical groups consider politics a secondary concern, and place a premium on staying out of politics or at least not becoming unalterably committed to one party. Consequently an important component of the solicitation of group support was the candidate's willingness to ask for this support. A number of candidates could not or would not ask for help, some of them trying and becoming reluctant after a few refusals. On the other hand, some candidates were willing to ask anybody for support and even to ask groups or people to withdraw their announced support for the opposing candidate. One such congressman, seeing a list of elected officials supporting his opponent, noticed two city councilmen on the list. He immediately called each of the men, reminded them of all that he had done for cities in his district, then suggested that perhaps they had been mistakenly listed. Both councilmen readily agreed and withdrew their endorsement publicly, much to the dismay of the challenger.

Candidates requesting support from a group are more likely to be successful if they already possess other campaign resources. One such resource is a political record or a political ideology that is acceptable to the group. Incumbents often indicated their ideology by referring to their records on bills that had already been before Congress, explaining the arguments for and against the bill and justifying their stand. Nonincumbents were more often expected to give specific and acceptable answers about issues yet to come before Congress. The reactions of groups to equivocal or general answers were illustrated by the appearance of one Democratic nonincumbent before a peace group. Near the conclusion of his answers, one woman rose from the audience and announced, "I'm tired of all this double talk. What we need is a candidate who is willing to stand up and be crucified." The candidate noted that he wanted to be elected, not crucified.

A resource which may be even more important than an acceptable ideology is vote-getting ability. Groups will often try to avoid alienating a likely winner, especially if they feel he may agree with their views on occasion. Furthermore, groups like to be able to indicate the importance of their endorsement by pointing to a record of past winners—candidates who were presumably assisted by their endorsement. In addition, as Nicholas Masters has pointed out, labor unions have endorsed candidates with whom they did not agree wholeheartedly because the popularity of these individuals made the entire slate of labor-endorsed candidates appear more acceptable to nonlabor voters.[7] Given these reasons, it is not surprising that Harry Scoble found that one group—labor unions—gave more support in 1960 to sure winners and less support to competitive candidates or sure losers than either the Democratic Senate Campaign Committee or the Republican National Campaign Committee. The distributions of financial support to strong, competitive, and weak candidates were as shown in Table 1.[8]

TABLE 1

Distribution of Organizational Campaign Funds by Candidate Strength (Percent)

Percent of Vote Received by Candidates	Democratic Committee	Republican Committee	Labor Unions
Over 55	39	23	52
46 through 54	45	52	37
Less than 46	16	25	11
	100	100	100

Source. See text, footnote 8.

However, this pattern of support for sure winners was not characteristic of Bay Area labor unions. In the Bay Area the AFL-CIO Committee on Political Education had for some

[7] Nicholas Masters, "The Politics of Union Endorsement of Candidates in the Detroit Area," *Midwest Journal of Political Science*, I, 145 (1957).
[8] Harry Scoble, "Organized Labor in Electoral Politics: Some Questions for The Discipline," *Western Political Quarterly*, 16, 683 (1963). The categories are Scoble's and apparently were not meant to exclude any candidates who fell between "46 through 54" and "over 55 per cent."

time concentrated its support on nonincumbents who had some chance of success, then gradually reduced its support as the candidate proved his vote-getting ability by being elected and reelected. Three of the incumbent congressmen had had strong labor support when each congressman first ran, but labor gradually reduced its assistance as each of the men became more and more certain of reelection. In 1962, Bay Area labor organizations gave their strongest support to candidates in new districts and in swing districts represented by Republicans. The success of this technique was indicated by the fact that 2 of the 8 incumbents were former labor union officials, and 4 others were supported by at least some unions.

The pattern of support for sure winners, despite their political views, did appear to be true of Bay Area newspapers, based on their endorsements in 1960 and 1962 and on the comments of candidates. Liberal candidates could assume that liberal newspapers would endorse them before their first election or for their first reelection, that moderate papers would begin endorsing them in their third or fourth terms, and that more conservative papers would begin endorsing them later. In 1962, *The Oakland Tribune*, owned by the family of former Republican Senator William Knowland, endorsed (for the first time) a liberal Democrat who was then running for his tenth term.

A third resource of value in securing a group's support is the personal characteristics and personal contacts of the candidate. A candidate who is a member of a group or who has personal friendships with leaders of the group has a distinct advantage. Securing a group's support very frequently requires personal meetings, and meetings with personal friends are more likely to be profitable than meetings with strangers. In the Bay Area, labor leaders conceded that an important factor in the decision to support one candidate was that labor union officials lived near his home and knew him socially. Because of this importance, active candidates worked hard to make such contacts, utilizing such techniques as writing letters to newly elected group officers or appointing group officials to patronage or campaign positions.

The process of gaining support was not always predictable,

however, and the unpredictability was well illustrated by the comments of three different candidates about the endorsement process of one of the major metropolitan newspapers. One candidate complained that the editor of the newspaper had asked only one question during their interview — whether or not the candidate favored the graduated income tax, which the editor opposed. Another candidate was denied endorsement by the paper because he failed to make a courtesy call on the political editor, although he had made a special trip for that purpose only to find the political editor out of his office. A third candidate reported that he was told that his name had been omitted the first day because of a "typographical error," but the error was repeated and was never corrected. The candidate believed the "error" was made because he had not participated in a public service program that the newspaper's television station had requested. The process of gaining support from small newspapers also had some elements of unpredictability. Some of the editors confessed in interviews that they did not know who was running; nevertheless, their newspapers endorsed candidates.

PATTERNS OF SUPPORT

Those Bay Area candidates who successfully asked for assistance from groups received not only endorsements but also money, workers, and access to members. The money was helpful but not in itself sufficient. Major contributions from a group might total $3000 to $5000, but much more common was a total of $300 to $800, combining contributions of all members of the group. Those amounts helped but were scarcely sufficient for $20,000 to $50,000 campaigns. Similarly, groups provided some but not enough workers. Perhaps the largest single sustained contribution of workers was by peace groups to the campaign of John O'Connell and, even here, the groups claimed only to have contributed one third of his workers. Probably as important as anything was the initial thrust to a political career that a group could give. One congressman, for example, was appointed to his first political office upon the recommendation of leaders of the Farm Bureau, in which he had been active. Another congressman, a labor union official, was given an uncontested party nomination in his first contest because he could get more assistance from the labor unions than could other prospective candidates.

Many groups are bipartisan, but there are some long standing differences in the types of groups from which the parties secure support. Previous studies have noted that Democrats are much more likely than Republicans to secure support from labor, with Republicans usually constituting 5 percent or less of the labor-supported candidates. Even when some unions endorse and support a Republican, other labor unions often give greater support to the opposing Democratic candidate.[9] Business groups support both Democrats and Republicans but usually give far more support to Republicans. Alexander Heard noted a difference in the type of businesses that have contributed money to each party, with Republicans receiving proportionately greater support from bankers, brokers, manufacturers, and officials in oil, mining, and utility companies. Democrats received proportionately greater support from distillers, merchants, makers of soft drinks, contractors, builders, publishers, and officials in building materials, radio, advertising, and amusement firms.[10] These general divisions of group support were repeated in the Bay Area. Labor favored Democrats highly. Two incumbent Republicans received some help from a few labor unions, but each of their opponents received far more help from other unions. Doctors supported Republican candidates heavily, while business leaders divided their support, showing a preference especially for incumbents. Peace groups were active in 1962, supporting Democratic nonincumbents and especially John O'Connell.

Compared to nonincumbents, incumbents held more of the resources valuable in securing group support, resulting in

[9]*Ibid.*, p. 684; See also Mary G. Zon, "Labor in Politics," *Law and Contemporary Problems*, **27**, 242 (1962).
[10]Alexander Heard, *The Costs of Democracy*, University of North Carolina Press, Chapel Hill, 1960, p. 124.

greater success in use of each of the techniques available. Incumbents had proved their vote-getting abilities, while many nonincumbents were making their first try for office. Incumbents had made political records by their votes on bills but nonincumbents were unknown quantities. Incumbents had many more personal contacts, having worked for many years to establish and maintain these contacts in the district and having been unable to avoid similar contacts with lobbyists in Washington D.C. Consequently, incumbents secured formal endorsements from more groups and personal endorsements or help from more group leaders. In asking for group endorsements, incumbents often did little more than note that they had received the group's endorsement in 1960, that they had since achieved two more years of seniority, and that they were continuing to try to represent all of the people as best they could. (In other words, incumbents often made no special appeal in their public statements to groups but, in fact, maintained that they were representing all citizens, not just particular groups.) In contrast nonincumbents who hoped to win endorsements needed to prepare speeches detailing their own views and the ways in which the incumbent had been deficient in representing the group's interests.

Incumbents were also more frequently allowed to make direct appeals to group members. Congressmen were frequently invited to present reports on the last congressional session to civic clubs and other nonpolitical groups. Nonincumbents who wished to speak about issues before Congress were often denied the right to do so because club rules prohibited "partisan" talks. Some groups even held special meetings to allow congressmen to speak to their members. For example, postal employees, who are restricted by the Hatch Act in their political participation, held some banquets at which incumbents were asked to speak. At the banquet for one Republican congressman, the master of ceremonies apologized for the limited attendance of only 50, but noted that all postal employees in the district had received at least one notice of the meeting, and that each notice indicated clearly that the congressman had always given strong support to their requests. Few direct appeals to members of a group could be more effective than that.

72 Acquiring The Support of Nonparty Groups

If incumbency is held constant, Republicans had some advantage over Democrats in making appeals to group memberships, probably because the people most likely to belong to groups — people with higher income and education — were likely to be Republicans. For example, civic clubs were more likely to allow a nonincumbent Republican to give a nonpolitical talk than a nonincumbent Democrat. Retired Admiral L. V. "Mike" Honsinger, a Republican, gave 50 speeches to civic groups on the Polaris missile, although he noted that his congressional candidacy was not mentioned nine tenths of the time. In contrast, one Democratic nonincumbent stated that he was not allowed to speak at any civic clubs in his district except in one city, a city so strongly Democratic in its culture that most of the businessmen were Democrats.

The advantages held by incumbents and Republicans in making direct appeals were well illustrated by the activities of three candidates who were observed trying to meet working people in their place of work. The first, who was both Republican and incumbent, met working people by arranging for company officers to take him from one factory work bench to another, usually accompanied by the foreman responsible for that area. The second, a Democratic state legislator, did not visit factories but was allowed to tour such public and semipublic offices as the state highway department and the telephone company, usually unaccompanied. The third, a Democratic nonincumbent, was allowed to do no more than stand outside factory gates at 5:30 in the morning, distributing literature under the watchful eye of a plant security officer.

Differences between sure winners and sure losers are easily predictable given the importance of vote-getting ability and the advantages of incumbents, who made up most of the sure winners. In addition, a difference in the number of personal contacts was indicated by the number of organizations in which candidates were active. Sure winners and competitive candidates often belonged to 10 or 20 organizations, while sure losers were more likely to belong to only a few. Having many advantages, sure winners won the endorsements of numerous groups, while sure losers won few. The greatest distinction between sure winners and sure losers was reached in one San Francisco district where the Democratic incumbent, a sure winner, had kept for many years a file on every group within the city that endorsed candidates, making certain that one of his campaign workers was at every endorsing session. At the end of the campaign, his manager proudly reported that the congressman had won the endorsement of every endorsing group in the city except those directly affiliated with the Republican party. One of the costs of the endorsements was evident in the applications for membership in some of the groups (and initiation fees) that the manager was then preparing for the congressman.

SUMMARY

Groups provide candidates with some votes, workers, and money. The amount, type, and value of support from each group depended on the resources it had, such as money, manpower or prestige, and its interest in politics. The principal techniques for winning support are compiling a suitable record, asking for assistance from group leaders or from members, and asking for or purchasing endorsements. Candidates requesting support were more likely to be successful if they already possessed other resources, specifically an acceptable political record on issues, vote-getting ability, and personal contacts. Incumbents and sure winners were more successful in securing group support than their counterparts, given the importance of prior possession of other resources. If incumbency is controlled, Republicans had more success than Democrats, apparently because the people most likely to belong to groups are Republicans. In the Bay Area, labor unions were an important exception to normal group patterns, since they concentrated their support on nonincumbents, gradually reducing their support for incumbents they had already helped elect. The pattern had obviously been successful, judged by the characteristics of the congressional delegation. (National data indicate that most labor unions follow the normal group patterns of support for incumbents and sure winners.)

Chapter 6

ACQUIRING CAMPAIGN FUNDS[1]

How much money does a congressional candidate need? In 1962 the treasurer of the Democratic National Congressional Committee estimated that across the United States the average campaign *against stiff opposition* would cost $25,000 to $50,000 in big city districts, and $15,000 to $25,000 in suburban or rural districts.[2] The implication of less cost for campaigns with weaker opposition is relevant for incumbents,

---

[1]This chapter is based on analysis of the financial statements filed with the California Secretary of State, observation of the campaigns, and interviews with candidates, campaign managers, and campaign finance chairmen and treasurers. The financial statements, especially those from Republican incumbents, were fairly thorough, accurate, complete, and far more valuable than the reports filed by the same candidates with the Clerk of the House of Representatives. (The reports filed with the Clerk by the national-level party committees do seem to be fairly complete.) The degree of inaccuracy in the California reports appeared to increase with the total cost of the campaign. Inaccuracies included failure to report payments in kind, such as billboard space, free newspaper advertising and volunteer work, disguising of sources by such techniques as listing contributions from committees rather than individuals, and omission of information, including some sums that did not formally go through the campaign committee. For other discussions of the value of campaign financial statements as research data, see John P. White and John R. Owens, "Michigan Campaign Expenditure Reports as Research Data," *Papers of the Michigan Academy of Science, Arts and Letters*, **44**, 255–272 (1959); Leonard Rowe and William Buchanan, "Campaign Funds in California: What the Records Reveal," *California Historical Society Quarterly*, 41, 195–210 (1962); Alexander Heard, *The Costs of Democracy*, Chapel Hill, University of North Carolina Press, 1960, pp. 359–370. Heard commented at length (pp. 4–5) on the lack of data on campaign financing, but such information is much more easily available and generally more accurate than information on the acquisition of workers, issues, groups, and other important campaign resources.

[2]*The Machinist*, April 29, 1962, p. 4, as quoted in Charles Clapp, *The Congressman: His World As He Sees It*, Brookings Institution, Washington, D.C., 1963, p. 340.

but not for challengers. Since votes will usually be cast in normal patterns in the absence of strenuous efforts to change those patterns, incumbents can expect to win elections in which they have only limited opposition. As a result, their financial needs are determined by the opposition and may oftentimes be fairly low. Candidates challenging incumbents (in congressional general elections, these challengers make up 80 percent or more of the noncumbents) usually have a chance to win only if they conduct expensive campaigns. As a result, the needs of noncumbents are usually high and almost always higher than those of incumbents.

In the Bay Area, candidates with stiff opposition, both incumbent and nonincumbent, felt that they needed about $50,000 to $60,000, a figure higher than that estimated by the treasurer of the Democratic National Congressional Committee. In contrast, sure winners usually found that $20,000 to $30,000 was sufficient to assure an easy victory.[3]

As a general rule, not only were the needs of incumbents less than those of nonincumbents, but also the longer an incumbent had served the less money he needed.[4] Incumbents needed less money because they wasted less money than nonincumbents. The President's Commission on Campaign Costs has reported: "Most politicians agree that half of campaign expenditures are wasted, but none knows which half."[5] In the Bay Area, incumbents appeared to have a much better idea than nonincumbents about which expenditures fell into the wasted half, and incumbents were thus less likely to spend for unprofitable items. One reason was that

[3] These figures are distinctly higher than the figures mentioned by congressmen across the nation. Clapp, *op. cit.*, pp. 335–338. This comparison and the comparison with the figures suggested by the treasurer of the Democratic National Committee indicates that California congressional compaigns are more expensive than those in many other parts of the nation. For an extensive study of California campaign financing, see Leonard Rowe, "Political Campaign Funds in California," unpublished Ph.D. dissertation, University of California, Berkeley, 1957.
[4] For a detailed comparison of the amounts needed and the length of service, see David Leuthold, "Electioneering in a Democracy: Congressional Election Campaigns in the San Francisco Bay Area 1962," unpublished Ph.D. dissertation, University of California, Berkeley, pp. 156–158.
[5] Quoted in Clapp, *op. cit.*, p. 350.

incumbents had dropped expenditures which they had used in the past but found unproductive. Incumbents were not confident that even in 1962 their money was spent efficiently but they did feel fairly certain that some of the expenditures they had dropped were not efficient. Most the expenditures that were dropped related to characteristics of the local district or the candidate, such as the finding of one candidate that fourfifths of the bumper stickers he had purchased two years before were still in the headquarters at the end of the campaign. In 1962 he ordered only a small number of stickers.

Another reason for less waste was that contributions to incumbents were more timely than contributions to nonincumbents. A campaign could be planned more rationally if contributions were available when needed. For example, nonincumbent L. V. "Mike" Honsinger lost the opportunity to use billboards because he did not have sufficient money available for the down payment on September 1, although the money arrived later. Some candidates borrowed money to overcome this lack of timeliness, but borrowing of this kind was risky for a nonincumbent who had never previously tested his ability to attract contributions. Although few data are available on the comparative timeliness of contributions for incumbents and nonincumbents, a study of 1960 reports filed with the House of Representatives did show that the Bay Area candidates who had received one third of their total contributions from national-level committees by September 1 included 100 percent of the incumbents but only 25 percent of the nonincumbents.[6]

Finally incumbents needed less money than nonincumbents because they received some services free. The franking privilege for mailings of "noncampaign" materials was worth several thousand dollars to at least one congressman. Almost all incumbents used some of the members of their government-paid office staff as campaign managers or assistants, a privilege worth $2000 or more.

[6]Compiled from reports in *Congressional Quarterly Weekly Report*, 1961, pp. 1059ff.

AMOUNTS RAISED

Nonincumbents may have needed more money but they found it harder to raise, and ended up with less money than incumbents. Comparative financial reports for 19 Bay Area general election congressional contests from 1958 to 1962 indicate that incumbents had the most money in 12 contests, challengers had the most in 4, and the 2 had approximately equal amounts in 3 contests.[7] This finding is similar to the usual finding that the incumbent party can more easily raise funds, other things being equal, but it is contrary to the views, reported by Charles Clapp, of a group of congressmen who unanimously agreed that their opponents always outspent them,[8] an extraordinary assertion to say the least.

The amount of money that could be raised depended not only on incumbency, but also apparently on the election year. More money was available for Bay Area congressional candidates in 1960, a presidential election year, than in 1958 or 1962, midterm election years. Judged by campaign financial statements, Bay Area incumbents had more money to spend in 1960 than in either 1958 or 1962, and the men who opposed them in 1960 had more money available than did the challengers of 1958 or 1962. The greater financing available in presidential years may be because people become more interested in politics then and are more willing to give, or it may be because California congressional candidates do not have to compete for funds with gubernatorial and other state-level candidates in presidential election years. Two Democratic candidates did complain that they had difficulty collecting funds in 1962 because their supporters wanted to contribute heavily to Governor Brown's campaign. Similarly, a Republican campaign manager noted that contributors to

[7]Reports in the files of the Secretary of State. As is shown in Table 1 of this chapter, incumbents and challengers were, on the average, more nearly even in 1962 than in previous years, with the reasons apparently being reapportionment, the death of one congressman during the campaign and the subsequent reduction of his expenditures, and the miscalculation and consequent overspending by one challenger.
[8]Clapp, *op. cit.*, pp. 343–344.

the local United Republican Finance Committee were allowed to designate their contribution for a specific candidate if they wished. In 1962 the congressman ranked third in these designations, behind gubernatorial candidate Richard Nixon, who was a heavy favorite, and the candidate for Attorney General. In 1964, the congressman ranked first, well ahead of Goldwater.

The location of the district was also important, because more money was available in some areas than in others. Specifically, more money was available in San Francisco and San Mateo counties than in the rest of the Bay Area, and the campaigns of the congressmen who represented these areas were well-financed. Most of the well-financed campaigns outside these areas were those in which candidates were willing and able to contribute handsomely to their own campaigns. The pattern had also been true in 1960. Of the Bay Area's major contributors to the Democratic party that year, 75 percent gave a San Francisco address. Of the major contributors to the Republican party, 60 percent gave a San Francisco address and 30 percent gave a San Mateo County address.[9]

SOURCES OF FUNDS

The 32 men who filed for the 1962 congressional elections in the Bay Area reported officially or unofficially total expenditures of slightly more than $750,000. If various unreported expenditures are added, the total cost of the 1962 primary and general election campaigns for 10 Bay Area congressional seats comes to about $1 million.

Financial reports filed by candidates allowed the classification of funds according to source, including (1) personal and family funds, (2) contributions collected by others, and

[9]*Congressional Quarterly Weekly Report*, loc. cit. Frank Kovac, finance director of the Draft Goldwater Committee similarly noted that the amount of money Goldwater received from any state in his 1964 prenomination campaign was in proportion to the amount of wealth there. Although Goldwater was disliked by many moderate and liberal New York Republicans, New York's contributions were second only to those of California. *The New York Times*, July 31, 1964, p. 10.

(3) contributions collected by the candidate or his finance committee. Table 1 presents data on the sources of funds for the 20 Bay Area candidates who campaigned in both the primary and general elections. The candidates are classified by party, incumbency, and competitiveness.

Table 1 shows that Democrats had more money than Republicans with the difference being the amount contributed by the candidates themselves.[10] Three Democratic nonincumbents and one Democratic incumbent made especially heavy personal contributions—amounts between $25,000 and $100,000 or more. To some extent the success of a political party depends upon its ability to attract candidates who are willing to commit significant personal resources in order to be elected. The plight of the Republican party is indicated by the fact that all four of these Democrats had been raised in Republican families. One had even been California president of the Young Republicans before switching allegiances.

While the reported personal contributions seemed high, there were many hidden personal contributions that were not disclosed by the financial statements. One of the most significant was the loss of income suffered by nonincumbents while they were campaigning. For example, L. V. "Mike" Honsinger declined a $37,000-a-year position to run for Congress. If he had taken this position, his income during the time he was campaigning for Congress would have been about $25,000. The loss of income for other candidates was not as great, but it still constituted at least a few thousand dollars for several candidates.

An estimated $2000 to $4000 was incurred for hidden living expenses by active candidates. These expenses in-

[10]Two other bits of data also indicate that among those who are involved in California politics, Democrats contribute more than Republicans. Among Bay Area campaign workers surveyed in 1962, 9 percent of those who worked for Democratic candidates claimed to have contributed money to the campaign compared to 3 percent of those who worked for Republicans. Similarly, Edmond Costantini found that California delegates to the 1960 Democratic national convention made larger contributions to the party in 1958 than did California delegates to the 1960 Republican national convention, even though the incomes of the Republicans were distinctly higher. *The Democratic Leadership Corps in California*, Institute of Governmental Affairs, University of California, Davis, 1967, pp. 23, 46.

TABLE 1

Amounts and Sources of Funds, Bay Area Congressional Candidates, 1962
(Averages for Primary and General Elections; Dollars)

Candidates	Personal and Family Contributions	Contributions Collected by Others	Contributions Collected by Candidate	Total Receipts
10 Republicans	1,100	7,300	15,700	24,100
10 Democrats	19,500	5,800	14,100	39,400
8 Incumbents	1,800	8,100	16,800	26,700
12 Nonincumbents	16,000	5,500	13,500	35,000
(8 Challengers	6,900	4,500	14,700	26,100)
(4 Candidates for open seats	34,300	7,600	11,100	53,000)
7 Sure winners	12,400[a]	6,400	13,200	32,000
6 Competitive Candidates	10,900	8,600	28,400	47,900
7 Sure losers	7,800	4,900	4,900	17,600
All 20 candidates	10,300	6,600	14,800	31,700

Source. Estimates based on interviews, reports filed by candidates, and observation of campaigns.

[a] Almost all of this amount was spent by one candidate in his primary campaign before he became a sure winner.

cluded the personal campaign expenses that candidates were expected to bear, usually including the cost of travel, meals, clothes, and the cleaning of clothes. One candidate commented that his home telephone bill tripled during the campaign; another had at least one monthly phone bill of $1000. If the candidate was young and his wife was helping, babysitting costs were high—for one candidate about $350 during the general election campaign. Some candidates were expected to buy tickets to party fund-raising affairs out of their own pockets. Finally, candidates tended to make significant purchases in order to create the proper impression. Two or three candidates purchased new cars for the campaign, and at least one candidate purchased a new house.

From the viewpoint of the candidate, campaign funds other than his own may be divided into two categories—those he collects himself or through his finance committee, and those that are collected by others and presented to him. The categorization is artificial in some ways, because some candidates' finance committees may operate so independently and so well that the candidate need spend little time collecting money. For this study, however, the assumption that all Bay Area candidates were actively involved in the fund-raising efforts of their committees seemed reasonable. Table 1 shows that, except for the differences between incumbents and their challengers, there were not large variations in the amounts that various types of candidates received from groups, with the average candidate being able to expect about $6600. For Democrats this money came about equally from party and labor sources. For Republicans it came principally from party sources but also from physicians.

Aside from this $6600 and the money of his own he wished to invest, the money a candidate needed was raised by him or by his finance committee. Such money came especially from individual people—friends, neighbors, party loyalists, and ideologues.

Incumbents held a significant advantage, for they had solicited contributions in the past, and one third to one half of the previous contributors would contribute again, judged by comparisons of names of contributors on campaign financial statements. In the Sixth District, Congressman William

Mailliard received contributions in 1962 from 40 percent of the people who had contributed to his campaign in 1960, and from 46 percent of the people who had contributed to his campaign in 1958. In contrast, only 13 percent of those people who had contributed to Mailliard's 1958 or 1960 opponents contributed to his 1962 opponent, John O'Connell. One nonincumbent overcame this recontribution disadvantage by recruiting his district's 1960 Democratic candidate as his finance chairman. As a result, approximately one third of the people who had contributed to the 1960 candidate contributed to the 1962 candidate. Another nonincumbent noted that the people who were most likely to respond to his appeals for money late in the campaign were the people who had given him money earlier in the campaign, indicating that it may not be necessary to wait two years for recontributions.

Three nonincumbent candidates commented that old friends had provided about $2000, while a fourth credited old friends with about $4000. These relatively small amounts, coupled with occasional comments from other candidates, indicated that in a large-scale campaign most of the contributors were, at best, only chance acquaintances of the candidate. A candidate apparently needs to be attractive enough to secure contributions from large numbers of people that he meets on the campaign trail.

For some candidates, an important source of individual contributions was those rich people who regularly gave large contributions to the party's candidates. A list that might include these people was compiled by drawing the names of all Bay Area people who contributed $500 or more to national level committees in 1960.[11] This list was compared with the lists of people who contributed to 1962 Bay Area congressional candidates. The comparison showed that the Democratic party did not have nearly as many rich contributors as the Republican party did, but that these few Democrats were more likely to contribute to several congressional campaigns than their Republican counterparts. Some Democratic families contributed to 5 or 6 local congressional campaigns, but only one Republican was found contributing to even 2 dif-

[11]*Congressional Quarterly Weekly Report, loc. cit.*

ferent campaigns. Some individuals and families split their contributions. For example, an apparel manufacturer gave $1000 to Republican William Mailliard and $500 to Mailliard's opponent, Democrat John O'Connell.[12]
Some, possibly all, candidates received contributions from outside their districts. Three candidates listed addresses and amounts for their contributors on their statements, and two other campaign treasurers made estimates. Out-of-district contributions usually ranged from $4500 to $6000, bolstered in each case by contributions from national level party committees or from labor unions or other groups headquartered outside the district. Incumbents were more likely to receive out-of-district contributions than nonincumbents because they received more help from national level committees and because they were more widely known nationally.

PROCEDURES FOR ACQUIRING FUNDS

Techniques for raising money varied with the sources on which candidates relied. Three Democratic candidates simply wrote checks on their own bank accounts, which were often bolstered with borrowed money.[13] Most Republicans submitted a budget request to the party and four received almost all of their funds from the party.

Personal solicitation was very important. The solicitation had to be by the right people, and at least three sure losers were never able to get their fund-raising campaigns off the ground because they could not get a prominent person to act as chairman of their fund-raising committee. Some campaign workers helped collect money, with 6 percent[14] of

[12]Alexander Heard discusses such split-ticket giving which occurs fairly often, in *op. cit.*, pp. 58-67.
[13]One unsuccessful candidate ended the campaign owing the bank $26,000, a substantial sum, considering his salary of $8500 per year.
[14]This percentage is far below the 55 percent reported among 1956 general election workers in the Los Angeles area, although much of the difference may be due to the different types of samples drawn. Dwaine Marvick and Charles Nixon, "Recruitment Contrasts in Rival Campaign Groups," *Political Decision-makers*, Dwaine Marvick, ed., The Free Press, Glencoe, 1961, p. 201. As in the Bay Area, Democratic campaign workers were more likely to collect funds than were Republicans.

those that were surveyed writing a note stating this on their questionnaire. The percentages of workers who collected funds, by categories of candidates, were as follows:

<table>
<tr><td colspan="2" align="center">*Percent*</td></tr>
<tr><td>Incumbent</td><td>4</td></tr>
<tr><td>Nonincumbent</td><td>10</td></tr>
<tr><td>Sure winners</td><td>4</td></tr>
<tr><td>Competitive</td><td>6</td></tr>
<tr><td>Sure losers</td><td>9</td></tr>
<tr><td>Democrats</td><td>9</td></tr>
<tr><td>Republicans</td><td>3</td></tr>
</table>

These figures indicate that the candidates who found it more difficult to raise money asked more of their campaign workers to help raise money.

Some candidates tried mail appeals, but the usual result was that the number of contributions received was barely enough to cover the cost of the mailing. Incumbents appeared to have much greater success with mail appeals than nonincumbents. Campaign meals were a frequent source of funds, at least 10 dinners, lunches, barbeques, or picnics being sponsored by Bay Area congressional candidates. The net profit ranged from $500 to $4000, the median being $1500. These affairs were used by all types of candidates with the only variations being that Democrats sponsored more than Republicans (8 to 2) and East Bay candidates sponsored more than San Francisco, San Mateo, and Marin County candidates (7 to 3). These 2 groups, Democrats and East Bay candidates, usually found fund raising more difficult than their counterparts did, indicating that dinners were used especially by candidates who found that personal solicitation and mail appeals were not productive enough.

Most candidates found fund raising very difficult. The advantages of a long-term incumbent were candidly expressed by one congressman who said that he had had great difficulty raising money when he first ran for Congress, but that now, after nine terms, he did not need to solicit at all. In fact, he found that he got larger contributions if he just waited for people to send them in than if he asked for them. He mentioned a call from one businessman who asked how much he needed. The congressman replied that $500 would be fine. "Oh hell," the businessman replied, "We'll get together a thousand dollars and send it over."

SUMMARY

The problems encountered in acquiring campaign finances depended, first of all, upon the amount needed. Nonincumbents almost always needed $50,000 to $60,000 but incumbents could expect to win with much less money, as long as they were not seriously challenged. Even in similar circumstances, incumbents had an advantage, since they wasted less money, received more timely contributions, and received more free services.

Nevertheless, incumbents raised money more easily than nonincumbents did. Similarly, Republicans raised it more easily than Democrats, and candidates in wealthy districts raised it more easily than those in poor districts. Incumbents, Republicans, and candidates in wealthy districts were likely to be able to raise sufficient money with a mail appeal and a fairly active campaign by a finance committee. Nonincumbents, Democrats, and candidates in poor districts were more likely to be forced into such relatively unsatisfactory techniques as campaign dinners, asking their workers to raise funds, and contributing heavily themselves. One of the advantages of the incumbents was that they were able to ask for money from contributors in previous campaigns, and one third to one half of these people contributed again. In the end, challengers averaged as much as the incumbents, but to do so they had to personally contribute an average of $5000 more to their campaigns. Similarly, Democrats had about $15,000 more than Republicans, but they also contributed, on the average, $18,000 more of their own funds to their campaign.

Chapter 7

SECURING CAMPAIGN WORKERS

Campaign workers are valuable for two reasons: they assist the candidate in securing and distributing campaign resources,[1] and they influence their friends, neighbors, and relatives. Several studies of the effect of precinct worker activity have concluded that an active precinct worker can change his precinct's division of the two-party vote in a presidential or congressional election by about 5 percentage points. His influence in primary elections and issue elections would probably be much greater.[2]

Observation of Bay Area campaigns indicated that for convenience of analysis, campaign workers could be divided into two categories: professionals and amateurs. The differences between the two involved not only skill but also amount of time dedicated to the campaign, ability and willingness to work with little prior notice, and sufficient familiarity with the campaign strategies and personnel to be able to work with limited supervision. The differences, as defined here,

---

[1] The need for workers was reduced in some Bay Area campaigns by the use of machines. In one Bay Area campaign, postcards were addressed by electronic equipment, providing fast enough service to address and place in the mail 110,000 postcards 5 days after they were received from the printer. In another district a candidate rented machines that played a recorded telephone message from the candidate to the voter after a worker had dialed the voter's number. In 10 days, 10 people made 90,000 calls, using these machines.

[2] Peter H. Rossi and Phillips Cutright, "The Impact of Party Organization in an Industrial Setting," *Community Political Systems*, Morris Janowitz, ed., The Free Press, Glencoe, 1961, pp. 81–116; Daniel Katz and Samuel J. Eldersveld, "The Impact of Local Party Activity Upon the Electorate," *Public Opinion Quarterly*, **25**, 1–24 (1961); Phillips Cutright, "Measuring the Impact of Local Party Activity on the General Election Vote," *Public Opinion Quarterly*, **27**, 372–386 (1963). For the greater variation in an issue election, see Raymond E. Wolfinger, "The Influence of Precinct Work on Voting Behavior," *Public Opinion Quarterly*, **27**, 387–398 (1963).

did not include pay, and both professionals and amateurs could be paid or unpaid.

PROFESSIONAL CAMPAIGN WORKERS

Professionals are people who are able and willing to work hard in political campaigns and are capable, because of the skills, knowledge, and acquaintances they possess, of doing campaign work of high quality with little assistance or supervision. Examples would include political bosses, some political appointees, some employees or directors of campaign management firms, and a few housewives. The most important and most studied professionals in California are the campaign management firms. For a fee these firms will take most of the responsibility of a campaign, usually providing competent direction. Everett Kindig, who made a study of California firms, noted that some of the top firms have enviable success records in the campaigns they have managed for propositions and candidates. Whitaker and Baxter won 74 of the 80 campaigns they managed between 1933 and 1958; Baus and Ross won 34 of 38 in 14 years; and Harry Lerner went 10 years without defeat. The firms concerned themselves especially with strategy and organization, and they emphasized their special skills in using mass media and influencing the public. The parties differed in their approach to the firms. Republicans, who used the firms more, adopted a business-like attitude and looked for ability and experience. Democrats were more concerned about the firm's ideological attitudes and history of party support. Kindig also noted that Democrats were less likely than Republicans to give the firms full control of the campaign, and that freshmen candidates were more willing to take advice from the firms than veterans were.[3]

Three Bay Area candidates hired professional campaign

[3]Everett W. Kindig, "The Professional Campaign: A Study of Political Public Relations Men in California Politics," unpublished Master's thesis, Stanford University, Stanford, 1962. See also Stanley Kelley, *Professional Public Relations and Political Power*, Johns Hopkins Press, Baltimore, 1956; and Robert J. Pitchell, "The Influence of Professional Campaign Management Firms in Partisan Elections in California," *Western Political Quarterly*, 11, 278–300 (1958).

management firms in 1962, two congressmen using the firms which had managed their previous campaigns. Apparently the firms charged about $7500 *plus* the 15 percent commission on advertising, which was deducted from the amounts paid to the media, *plus* expenses. (These fees restricted usage of the firms to those campaigns in which substantial financial resources were sure to be available, thus helping to account for the success of the firms.) The firms usually relieved the candidates of numerous problems that would otherwise have slowed them and their campaigns. The firms had sufficient skill to recognize the necessities for a successful campaign and the pitfalls to be avoided. That the firms could be well worth their fee was indicated by the rehiring of firms by two congressmen. That some might not be worth their fee was indicated by the experience of the nonincumbent who found that officials of the campaign firm seldom came to the headquarters, and then usually with advice that the candidate considered poor.

Several candidates hired a campaign manager rather than a campaign management firm, picking people with experience in news media, advertising, party affairs, or local campaigns. Fees for these managers apparently ranged from $2500 to $4500 per campaign, sometimes including services of the manager's secretary. As a rule, these managers had less experience and skill than the campaign management firms — it was the first congressional campaign that any of them had run. Most of them, however, were willing to put more time into the campaigns than the campaign management firms were willing to put, and some of these managers were more familiar with the local political situation than were the firms.

The most inexpensive and efficient procedure was that followed by most of the congressmen — use of their field secretaries as campaign managers or managers-without-portfolio. Congressmen have varying arrangements with their field secretaries about the amount of work required and the amount of outside activity allowed. In some cases, field secretaries were allowed to operate advertising agencies, handling some commercial accounts and managing some campaigns, usually noncontroversial or nonpartisan campaigns that would not interfere with the congressman's campaign. These agencies usually handled advertising for the congressman's campaign, in many cases without charge. The return of the 15 percent advertising commission to the campaign treasury thus resulted in lower advertising costs for these incumbents than for other candidates. Most of the field secretaries who did not own advertising firms had special campaign skills, such as ability to prepare mailings or press releases or to locate places for campaign signs. Most field secretaries brought to their campaigns a high level of political skill, a detailed knowledge of the local political situation and the congressman's attitudes, and a willingness to work long hours. Since most of them did not charge any fee, they were excellent bargains.

As noted earlier, some unpaid people may be considered as professionals if they contribute a great deal of high quality work. In the Bay Area these people usually fit into one of two categories: (1) fund raisers who had collected funds for this candidate or other candidates in the past and knew how and from whom to raise money, and (2) skilled people who were loyal to their party, and who, through participation in campaigns year after year, had become expert in numerous procedures. The latter group included a number of lawyers, some housewives, and some wives of candidates. The skills and resources of these people included such things as the ability to set up and run a headquarters or a precinct organization, the knowledge of where and how to order campaign materials, and acquaintances with people who could provide important support.

AMATEUR CAMPAIGN WORKERS

Amateur campaign workers are more likely than professionals to work on a part-time basis and to have less ability. Usually they are unpaid. Many precinct committeemen would fit into this category but, more commonly, at least in California, amateurs are people who ring a few doorbells and help get out a mailing. Several studies have found that in a presidential or midterm election year about 3 to 5 percent of the adult population engage in some sort of campaign work. About 8 to 13 percent claim to have worked in at least one campaign in the past.[4]

Information about Bay Area amateur campaign workers was secured by a mail survey of workers for the candidates. Lists of workers were provided by 19 of the 20 candidates but they varied from campaign to campaign, including or excluding, for example, people who were hired, party precinct workers in the district, people who put up signs in front of their houses, and people who worked only on election day. Nevertheless the lists had some validity because they included the people whom the candidate thought of as his campaign workers. Because the lists varied in size, all names were taken from lists with less than 100 names, but only a sample of names (usually about 50) were taken from the larger lists. The two-page questionnaires were mailed to more than 900 workers in May 1963, and about 60 percent returned usable replies.[5] The reader unfamiliar with survey practices should realize that some of these procedures are short cuts, so that there is a higher probability of error in this survey than would be true for many academic surveys. An encouraging indication of accuracy however is the fact that findings from the survey were corroborated in many cases by observation of the campaigns and conversations with campaign workers.

The number of workers listed for campaigns ranged from less than 20 to more than 1000, varying with the amount of

[4] Angus Campbell, Philip E. Converse, Warren E. Miller, and Donald E. Stokes, *The American Voter*, John Wiley and Sons, New York, 1960, p. 91; Robert E. Lane, *Political Life: Why People Get Involved in Politics*, The Free Press, Glencoe, 1959, pp. 53–54; Robert A. Dahl, *Who Governs?*, Yale University Press, New Haven, 1961, p. 278; Julian L. Woodward and Elmo Roper, "Political Activity of American Citizens," *American Political Science Review*, **44**, 872–885 (1950); Samuel J. Eldersveld, *Political Parties: A Behavioral Analysis*, Rand McNally, Chicago, 1964, p. 19.

[5] The questionnaire is included in Appendix B. For a full description of the samples, see David A. Leuthold, "Electioneering in a Democracy: Congressional Election Campaigns in the San Francisco Bay Area 1962," unpublished Ph.D. dissertation, University of California, Berkeley, 1965, pp. 191–192 and 312–317.

activity in the campaign and the number of party precinct workers available. (In the campaign with the fewest workers, one person who volunteered in midsummer was told by the candidate, "Congratulations, you're the first to volunteer and so you're the campaign chairman.") As important as the quantity was the quality. One campaign manager with several hundred workers commented discouragingly: "I'm not sure but what 7 full-time personable, efficient people couldn't have done just as much as that whole volunteer group as far as precinct work goes."[6] A successful campaign manager with only 27 workers pointed out that "We actually didn't need any more. People worked hard and we had a good tight little ship."

The average number of workers for various categories of candidates was as follows.

	Workers
Incumbents	345
Nonincumbents	320
Sure winners	240
Competitive	600
Sure losers	175
Democrats	450
Republicans	220
All candidates	330

Democratic congressional candidates had more workers than Republicans but part of the reason was that Democrats often had to recruit precinct workers to compensate for their nonexistent official party organization. Competitive candidates had the largest average number of workers; sure winners did not need as many, and sure losers could not attract as many.

[6] An important consideration in the number of workers needed was the amount of work that each did. A comparison of the total number of pieces of mail sent and the number of workers who claimed to have worked on mailings indicated that the number of pieces of mail, prepared by the average worker who helped with mailings, varied from 200 to 800 in the different campaigns.

Workers were asked to estimate the number of hours they had worked for their candidates, and there were no significant differences in the averages for the various categories of candidates.

The relative importance, for different types of candidates, of three potential sources — friends of the candidate, members of political clubs, and workers from previous campaigns — is indicated in Table 1. (Some people may of course be in all three of these groups, or they may have come to work for the candidate for reasons unrelated to these factors, but the proportions of campaign workers which do fit into each category give some clues about their possible importance as sources.) Overall the largest category was political club members, more than half of the workers belonging to some political club, such as the CDC or a Republican Women's Club. The smallest category was friends of the candidate, less than one fifth of the workers having been friends of the candidate before the campaign. This figure illustrates once again the need for candidates to secure help from large numbers of people that they meet on the campaign trail. Table 1 indicates, however, that friends can provide an initial base of support for all types of candidates. The addition of workers from previous campaigns tips the scales substantially in favor of incumbents and thus to sure winners and competitive candidates as well.

Data from national surveys have indicated that campaign workers are better educated than the public as a whole, and have higher incomes, higher social status, and higher-level occupations.[7] This was also true of Bay Area campaign workers. About 50 percent of the campaign workers were college graduates, compared to 12 percent of the Bay Area population. About 25 percent of the campaign workers had family incomes of $15,000 per year or more compared to 7 percent of the Bay Area families.[8] These education and income levels

---

[7] Based on analysis of data from the 1952 national survey conducted by the Survey Research Center, University of Michigan.
[8] James Sandmire surveyed members of county central committees in the Bay Area and found even higher levels of education and income. "The Politics of Disinterest: An Analysis of the County Central Committees of the San Francisco Bay Area," typewritten manuscript in library of Institute of Governmental Studies, University of California, Berkeley, 75 pp.

TABLE 1
Numbers of Campaign Workers from Various Sources

Categories of Candidates	Average Number of Workers Who Were:		
	Friends of Candidate	Political Club Members	Workers for Candidate in Previous Campaign for Any Office
Democrats (9)[a]	100	280	100
Republicans (10)	30	90	60
Incumbents (8)	70	170	160
Nonincumbents (11)[a]	55	175	25
Sure winners (6)[a]	60	120	120
Competitive (6)	70	300	110
Sure losers (7)	40	110	10
All candidates	65	175	80

Source. Lists of campaign workers provided by candidates and responses to questionnaires sent to campaign workers. In some cases, estimates were made, based on information provided by candidates and observation of campaigns.
[a]One candidate refused to provide a list of workers.

seemed to depend upon district characteristics with the highest average incomes and educations being found in the suburban and middle-class districts likely to be represented by Republicans and the lowest being in working class districts represented by Democrats. In each type of district the characteristics of workers for the losers were somewhat similar to characteristics of workers for the winners. Overall, however, workers for Republicans were older and had higher incomes, while workers for Democratic candidates had higher educations. Workers for incumbents were older and a little less educated than those for nonincumbents.

Political Orientation

The political orientation of campaign workers differs from the general public in level and direction. As we would expect, campaign workers are much more interested in politics than the average citizen. If, however, we disregard the difference in levels of political interest, campaign workers are oriented more toward issues and less toward candidates and parties than the general public, judged by the reasons given for their vote decision. As noted earlier, respondents in the 1962 national survey were asked for the most important reasons for their voting decision in their district's congressional race. The proportion of reasons in each classification, for those who said they had worked for one of the parties or candidates and for those who had not, was as follows.[9]

	Campaign Workers (Percent)	General Public (Percent)
Candidate	27	45
Party	22	31
Issues	33	12
Group	7	5
Other (influence of relatives, etc.)	11	7
	100	100
Number of reasons	(45)	(759)

Other studies have reported that campaign workers, when asked directly why they have become active in politics, have mentioned political reasons most frequently, followed by civic, social, and economic reasons in that order. Among political reasons, party loyalty and concern with public issues were most important, followed by candidate orientation.[10] Some differences have been found between the parties in these political reasons. A southern California study showed that party loyalty was more important to Republican amateur workers, while concern with issues was more important to Democrats. The percentages for workers in each party were as follows.[11]

[9] Data from 1962 national survey conducted by Survey Research Center University of Michigan, made available by Inter-university Consortium for Political Research.
[10] See, for example, Dwaine Marvick and Charles Nixon, "Recruitment Contrasts in Rival Campaign Groups," *Political Decision-makers,* Dwaine Marvick, ed., The Free Press, Glencoe, 1961, p. 208; Eldersveld, *op. cit.*, p. 132; Sandmire, *op. cit.*, p. 35.
[11] Marvick and Nixon, *op. cit.*, p. 208.

	Republicans (Percent)	Democrats (Percent)
Strong party loyalty a very important reason for working	78	61
Concern with public issues a very important reason for working	71	83

The political orientation of Bay Area campaign workers appeared to be similar to that of workers across the nation. Judged by various answers, including comments added to the questionnaire, party and issue identification were quite important, candidate identification was mixed, and group identification was relatively unimportant. The importance of party loyalty was indicated by the fact that 72 percent[12] of the Bay Area workers considered themselves strong (rather than not-too-strong) members of their party compared to 35 percent in the 1962 national sample of the University of Michigan Survey Research Center. The strength of party loyalty did not differ among the workers for the various categories of candidates.

Campaign workers for incumbents were more likely to add candidate-oriented responses to their questionnaire than were those for nonincumbents. For each incumbent, there were some comments indicating high respect for his personal qualities. Just as common, however, were comments related to the incumbent's activities in office. A number of campaign workers noted that their candidate had helped them to get a government job or to process some claim through a bureaucracy. Some campaign workers admired their candidate because he kept the district informed by sending out good newsletters. Others said that they had met the incumbent when they toured Washington, D.C., and had been impressed by him. Among nonincumbents, admiration was expressed most frequently for L. V. "Mike" Honsinger, with a number of his campaign workers stating that they felt the only possible reason for his loss was that not enough voters

---

[12] About 2 percent of the Bay Area workers considered themselves strong members of the party opposite that of their candidate.

got "to know his qualifications."[13] Otherwise, comments about nonincumbents were mixed, some being kind and admiring, others indicating a gradually increasing disappointment in their candidate. The most disappointed of all referred to his candidate as "an inarticulate boob, and his own worst liability."

Some indications of varying attitudes toward issues were provided by worker answers to four questions which were combined to form a Role of the Federal Government Scale.[14] Workers for Democrats were of course more strongly in favor of an increased role than workers for Republicans. Within each party, however, workers for incumbents were more moderate than workers for nonincumbents, and workers for sure winners were more moderate than workers for sure losers. In other words, workers for Republican incumbents were less conservative than workers for Republican nonincumbents, and workers for Democratic incumbents were less liberal than workers for Democratic nonincumbents. Extremists are apparently alienated by the compromises to which most incumbents must agree, if they are to be effective.

An interaction between the appeal of an attractive candidate, the party to which a worker is loyal, and the issues the worker believes in was indicated by the analysis. This interaction, plus interview comments from some campaign workers, indicated that among the 3 to 5 percent of the adult population participating in a particular year are a fair number of regular party workers who volunteer to work for the candidate whose personality and issue-orientation most appeal to them that year. Similarly, in the reservoir of 5 to 10 percent more who participate now and then, are a fair number who are loyal to their party or are quite concerned with issues but work only if they find an attractive candidate who takes positions that they can enthusiastically support.

[13] Further evidence of the esteem held for Honsinger was provided by the fact that 850 people came to a Sunday afternoon reception in his honor just before the election.
[14] Respondents were asked if the following policies should be increased, left as is, or decreased: federal action to increase employment; federal programs for medical care for the aged; federal aid to education; federal action to decrease racial discrimination.

Recruiting Techniques

Workers could be recruited in a number of ways. Some workers, such as secretarial staffs and people to put up signs, could be hired, and others could be requested from groups such as labor unions or corporations. For the most part, however, just as with contributions, party support, and group support, it was necessary to solicit. Candidates had to be willing to ask people to work, and they had to be attractive enough to win affirmative responses even from new acquaintances. The best results were secured if the solicitations were made to people who were likely to say yes and if they came from a person important to the respondent. Telephone calls to lists of registered party voters were generally unproductive. One party worker making such calls commented that 14 hours on the telephone had netted only 3 workers. Stories filtered up from Southern California of a very effective lady in Orange County who secured people to cover 80 precincts by telephone calls during the summer. She was reported to have averaged a precinct worker for each hour of telephoning, and to have telephoned as much as 4 or 5 hours a day, a process that must have required amazing fortitude. Some candidates organized the process of recruiting workers by distributing pledge cards for would-be workers to sign. One such candidate reported that more than half of the people who had signed such cards helped in the campaign.

Candidates offered several incentives to prospective workers besides the salaries noted above. One of the most important was the opportunity to associate with influential people, especially the candidate. Another was the opportunity to learn about politics and government. Some candidates used social affairs. Robert Leggett was one of the most successful of these, holding numerous picnics, dinners, "bean feeds," and campaign breakfasts. The issue orientation of candidates attracted people who shared their attitudes; for example, many peace-oriented people worked for John O'Connell because he advocated reductions in the arms race. Another incentive was a title, a specific assignment, and responsibility. At least one candidate tried to use his power to appoint people to the party's state central committee as a means of securing campaign workers, but he was doomed to disappointment because his appointees lost their interest in his campaign once they had the appointments in hand. More effective patronage, which enticed a number of people, was the prospect of serving on a congressional staff, either in Washington, D.C., or in the district, or the prospect of securing support of party leaders for a later political candidacy by the campaign worker. Congressmen could also provide valuable services for constituents and, as already noted, a fair number of campaign workers for incumbents indicated that the congressman had helped them at some time in the past.

Many workers were unsatisfactory, and it was necessary to secure replacements for them. This was especially true of publicity men hired to write press releases or design materials, most of whom were too slow and too unfamiliar with politics. A number of other people did well but tired after a time and also needed to be replaced. These problems were much more serious for nonincumbents than for incumbents. Incumbents had tested people in previous campaigns and knew which people had the skills and stamina to do a job and which people would report truthfully if the job was not done. Consequently, incumbents relied as much as possible on the people who had performed well before; each campaign worker accepted the responsibility he had had two years before, and a working organization sprang into existence. Sure losers commented that their problem was complicated not only by the tendency of inexperienced workers to return to their own businesses before the end of the campaign but, even more, by the tendency for experienced campaign workers to leave them for campaigns with brighter prospects.

SUMMARY

The successful acquisition of workers requires first and foremost the acquisition, usually by hiring, of some professional campaign workers. Incumbents, who can use their field secretaries, have a substantial economic advantage over nonincumbents. The acquisition of amateur workers depends especially upon the ability of the candidate to influence middle-class party loyalists and political club members to work for him. These people will be interested especially in his personal characteristics and his issue-orientation. Once again incumbents had a significant advantage because they could secure about half of the workers they needed from their lists of workers in previous campaigns.

Chapter 8

USE OF RESOURCES — ACTIVITIES

Most of the studies of campaign activities have been journalistic and descriptive rather than analytical, one reason being the difficulty of classifying many diverse activities, much less trying to discover and explain variations. This diversity of activity exists in almost all campaigns. Former congressional candidate Stimson Bullitt has argued that the diversity is due to lack of knowledge:[1]

Because no one knows what works in a campaign, money is spent beyond the point of diminishing returns. To meet similar efforts of the opposition all advertising and propaganda devices are used — billboards, radio, TV, sound trucks, newspaper ads, letter writing or telephone committee programs, handbills, bus cards. No one dares to omit any approach. Every cartridge must be fired because among the multitude of blanks one may be a bullet.

On the other hand, Clem Whitaker, manager of many California campaigns, has argued that different procedures must be used because the candidate must gain a voter's attention seven times if he is to make a sale.[2] Whatever the reason, campaign activities are sufficiently diverse to make classification and analysis difficult.

One means of classification is the separation of activities (the subject of this chapter) from the content of the appeals made in each of the activities (the subject of the next chapter). All six resources are converted into either activities or appeals, or both. The candidate, party leaders, group mem-

---
[1] Stimson Bullitt, *What It Means To Be A Politician,* Anchor Books, Doubleday, Garden City, New York, 1961, p. 72.
[2] Everett Kindig, "The Professional Campaign: A Study of Political Public Relations Men in California Politics," unpublished Master's thesis, Stanford University, Stanford, 1962, p. 113.

bers, and workers may all be active, and money will be used to purchase advertising or workers. Appeals to voters will be based on a candidate's personal qualities, his party support, the issues he believes in, or the groups which are supporting him.

MEASURING ACTIVITIES

One means of measuring the activities of a campaign is by calculating the purposes for which funds are spent. In California, candidates are required to list their expenditures for various specified purposes on the financial reports they file with the California Secretary of State. In interviews, candidates commented that the information on distribution of expenditures was probably less accurate than the information on receipts of funds, because of the difficulty of classification, but the figures usually represented the candidates' best estimates. Comparison with other data, such as interview data about the size of mailings, indicated that the figures were reasonably accurate. Some comparisons may be made with figures represented by Alexander Heard, who compiled 1956 reports of 350 local-level committees in the 100 most populous counties in the United States.[3] The proportions of expenditures for various purposes were as follows:

	Bay Area Congressional Candidates, 1962 (Percent)	350 Local Committees, 1956 (Percent)
Printing, distributing, mailing literature, handouts	26	21
Newspaper, periodical advertising	13	9
Television, radio advertising	6	10
Billboards, signs	16	3
Other (election day expenses, overhead, etc. In the Bay Area personnel = 18%)	39	57
	100	100

[3]Alexander Heard, *The Costs of Democracy*, University of North Carolina Press, Chapel Hill, 1960, pp. 390-391.

The figures are fairly similar except for the higher amount spent for billboards and signs in the Bay Area, and the lesser amount spent for other activities. Even these differences may be based partially on the different systems of classification.

Another means of measuring campaign activities is by calculating the activities of campaign workers. The easiest procedure is by asking workers whether or not they engaged in particular activities,[4] and such questions were asked in the campaign worker survey. Some overstatement of activities is probable, based on misinterpretation of questions, and a biasing of responses toward active workers, both in the original sample and in those workers who responded. The proportions of workers who engaged in various activities were as follows:

	Percent
Talk to people to persuade them to vote for your candidate	88
Help get out a mailing to voters	64
Help get out the vote on election day	63
Help register voters	34
Do door to door canvassing	32

Additional written comments by workers indicated that the next most frequent activities, in descending order, were telephoning, arranging meetings, putting up posters, giving "coffees" in their homes, and giving speeches.

PARTY, COMPETITIVENESS, INCUMBENCY

These measurements may be used to compare the campaigns of Republicans and Democrats, of sure winners, competitive candidates and sure losers, and of incumbents and nonincumbents. Table 1 presents the average amount

[4] Such questions were asked in a survey of Southern California campaign workers, but the findings were influenced by the sample design. The sample of workers was drawn by a snowballing technique—interviewing people holding official or semiofficial party positions, then asking them to name key workers. All workers named by at least two people were interviewed. In this sample, about half of the respondents had engaged in coordinating, fund-raising, and strategy activities. Dwaine Marvick and Charles Nixon, "Recruitment Contrasts in Rival Campaign Groups," *Political Decision-makers*, Dwaine Marvick, ed., The Free Press, Glencoe, 1961, p. 201.

that each type of candidate spent for various purposes, and Table 2 presents the percentage of campaign workers who engaged in various activities for each type of candidate. One other measure of activity is the number of days that candidates spent campaigning. Including both the primary and general election campaigns, the averages were:

	Days
Incumbents	20
Nonincumbents	115
Sure winners	25
Competitive	150
Sure losers	80
Democrats	100
Republicans	60
All candidates	80

Much of the difference between incumbents and nonincumbents is due to the length of the congressional session, which kept incumbents in Washington until mid-October.

Party

The differences between the activities of Republicans and Democrats appear to be based on characteristics of their voters. Each party spent a significant proportion of its resources to reinforce the loyalties of party voters. Voter behavior studies have indicated that such a strategy is well chosen, considering the large number of party loyalists compared to the number of switchers, and the likelihood of greater success in getting out a party vote than in switching a vote from the other column.[5] Compared to Democrats, Republican voters are usually more highly educated, more likely to read newspapers and go to meetings, and more likely to vote with only limited urging. Consequently, it is not surprising that

---
[5]See for example Bernard R. Berelson, Paul F. Lazarsfeld, and William N. McPhee, *Voting: A Study of Opinion Formation in a Presidential Campaign*, University of Chicago Press, Chicago, 1954, p. 17. Only 16 percent of the respondents wavered between parties during the course of the campaign, but 28 percent failed to vote.

TABLE 1

Comparisons of Purposes of Expenditures, General Election

Average Percent of Expenditures (Average Dollar Amounts in Parentheses)

Class of Candidates	Personnel[a]	Signs, Billboards	Mailings and Handouts	Newspaper Ads	Radio and TV Ads	Other[b]	Total
All 20 candidates	18 (3,580)	16 (3,691)	26 (5,260)	13 (2,720)	6 (1,318)	21 (4,188)	100 (20,757)
10 Republicans	16 (3,065)	19 (3,519)	22 (4,167)	18 (3,428)	6 (1,169)	19 (3,490)	100 (18,838)
10 Democrats	19 (4,095)	15 (3,238)	29 (6,352)	9 (2,012)	7 (1,467)	22 (4,887)	101 (22,051)
8 Incumbents	16 (3,535)	14 (3,080)	27 (5,821)	16 (3,446)	9 (1,938)	17 (3,635)	99 (21,455)
12 Nonincumbents	18 (3,610)	18 (3,577)	25 (4,886)	11 (2,236)	5 (905)	23 (4,556)	100 (19,770)
7 Sure winners	15 (2,425)	18 (3,013)	31 (5,157)	19 (3,133)	1 (117)	17 (2,754)	101 (16,599)
6 Competitive	17 (5,824)	15 (4,977)	25 (8,496)	11 (3,640)	12 (3,966)	21 (7,253)	101 (34,156)
7 Sure losers	22 (2,811)	19 (2,373)	21 (2,589)	12 (1,519)	2 (250)	24 (2,995)	100 (12,537)

Sources. Compilations based on statements filed by candidates and their committees with the California Secretary of State, and on interviews.

[a]Includes some payments for voter registration and voter canvassing.
[b]Includes travel, headquarters, phone, office supplies, photos, and miscellaneous.

TABLE 2
Activities of Campaign Workers

	Persuade People		Activities Checked on Questionnaire[a]							
			Get Out Mailing		Get Out Vote		Register Voters		Doorstep Canvassing	
Categories of Candidates	Percent	Average Number	Percent	Average Number	Percent	Average Number	Percent	Average Number	Percent	Average Number
All 20 candidates	88	295	64	215	63	210	34	115	32	110
10 Republicans	86	190	66	145	58	130	28	60	23	50
10 Democrats	90	405	62	280	68	305	39	175	39	175
8 Incumbents	86	290	72	245	60	205	30	100	26	90
12 Nonincumbents	89	260	58	170	65	190	37	110	37	110
7 Sure winners	85	205	77	185	54	130	29	70	22	55
6 Competitive	88	530	60	360	68	410	33	200	32	190
7 Sure losers	92	160	53	95	65	115	43	75	43	75

Sources. Responses on questionnaire mailed to sample of campaign workers. Average numbers of workers performing each activity are computed by multiplying percentages times average number of workers for campaigns in that category, as presented in Table 1, Chapter 7.

[a] "Did you do any of the following?
1. "Talk to people to persuade them to vote for your candidate."
2. "Help get out a mailing to voters."
3. "Help get out the vote on election day."
4. "Help register voters."
5. "Do door to door canvassing."

Republicans spent a higher proportion of their funds for newspaper ads, signs and billboards, and that Republican workers were more likely than Democratic workers to arrange meetings at which their candidate spoke, or to give speeches themselves. Democratic voters were more likely to be stimulated to vote only by some form of personal contact. As a result, Democratic candidates spent a higher proportion of funds for personnel and mailings, and asked a higher proportion of their workers to register voters, go door to door, telephone, and get out the vote on election day.[6]

The differences are not entirely due to the characteristics of each party's voters. One reason that workers for Democratic congressional candidates spent more time in door-to-door type activities was because the regular Democratic precinct organizations were usually less effective than the regular Republican organizations. Another reason was that Democratic candidates made more of an effort to be competitive, and this was likely to affect worker activities. The greater efforts to be competitive were indicated by the much greater amounts of money that Democratic candidates contributed to their own campaigns and by the 40 extra days of campaigning put in by the average Democratic candidate (100 days average for Democrats, 60 for Republicans).

Competitiveness

The effort to be competitive produced psychological strain. Candidates agreed that personal contact was the most successful means of influencing voters,[7] but it also appeared that

[6]These findings correspond with some findings reported earlier by Alexander Heard. Expenditure patterns for local committees in Connecticut, Maryland, and Pennsylvania showed that Democrats spent, in each state, a greater proportion of their funds for election day activities and, in Maryland and Pennsylvania, a smaller proportion for publicity and propaganda. Heard, *op. cit.*, p. 393.
[7]For similar comments by legislative candidates in Texas, see David Olson, *Legislative Primary Elections in Austin, Texas 1962*, Public Affairs Series No. 54, Institute of Public Affairs, University of Texas, Austin, 1963, p. 62. For such comments by congressmen, see Charles Clapp, *The Congressman: His World as He Sees It*, Brookings Institution, Washington, D.C., 1963, p. 380. See also Peter H. Rossi and Phillips Cutright, "Party Organization in Primary Elections," *American Journal of Sociology*, 64, 266 (1958).

it was the most difficult campaign activity. This was especially true of personal contact with the relatively apathetic voters who were reached only in their homes rather than at a political meeting. Most challengers felt that they needed to ring doorbells in order to have a chance of being elected, while most sure winners and their workers avoided such activity if they possibly could. Workers for sure winners were less likely than workers for competitive candidates or sure losers to have been involved in getting out the vote, registering voters, going door to door, or telephoning—all psychologically difficult tasks. They were more likely, however, to have been involved in such psychologically easy tasks as getting out a mailing or arranging meetings at which their candidate would speak. Sure winners spent a higher proportion of their money for mailings and newspaper ads, and a lower proportion on personnel. The relative difficulty of the tasks required of workers helps to explain why sure losers had more difficulty recruiting and keeping workers than sure winners did, and why challengers needed lots of workers if they were to be competitive. This interpretation of campaign activities is also supported by the campaign histories of at least two of the sure winners. Both mentioned that they had gone door to door extensively in the campaign in which they had defeated an incumbent congressman to win their own seat, but neither went door to door in 1962, when both were sure winners.

Incumbency

The differences between incumbents and nonincumbents were often the differences between sure winners and sure losers. The campaign activities asked of workers for incumbents were less demanding than those asked of workers for nonincumbents. Workers for incumbents were more often asked to help get out a mailing or to arrange a meeting, while workers for nonincumbents were asked more often to do doorstep canvassing, voter registering, or telephoning. The differences were indicated in the contrasts of the campaign days of the candidates. Incumbents came to their office each morning and transacted congressional business through the day, meeting with constituents, and soliciting support from and giving help to important people. During the day the congressmen also spoke to a couple of groups of a hundred people each, visited one or more party campaign headquarters or dropped in at some meeting of party workers, gave a newspaper or television interview, conferred with top campaign officials, and attended some social affair. No incumbent went door to door and only one toured any manufacturing plants or shopping centers. In contrast, active nonincumbents tried to arrange a coffee at 10 o'clock, a luncheon talk about some nonpartisan subject at noon, and a visit with some group in the evening. The rest of the day was spent knocking on doors, visiting shopping centers, trying to make the myriad arrangements necessary for the new supply of handcards or the sign-posting party on Tuesday night, and attempting to learn about the program of federal aid to impacted school districts and the incumbent's attitude toward it.[8] Inactive nonincumbents spent the day at their business office and tried to go out in the evening to a coffee hour or some public event.

Because of the length of the congressional session, incumbents were able to avoid and postpone campaign activities, simultaneously remaining in the public spotlight and deny-

[8] To judge from the literature on political campaigns, the "typical" day of every candidate begins at 5:30 A.M. in front of some factory gate. In the Bay Area however, only one candidate greeted workers at a factory gate early in the morning. This failure of 19 of the 20 candidates to begin the day in the "traditional" manner indicates that candidates are human beings, subject to the same energy limitations as the rest of us. The stereotype of the active candidate is so strong however that it colors even the views of campaign managers. Most managers, when asked to suggest days on which the candidate might be observed, searched their calendars for the day on which he would be most active and then apologized afterwards for having selected a day when he "wasn't as busy as usual."

Even if the days did not meet the expectations of the stereotypes, they were still grueling, especially for nonincumbents. The problems of maintaining family relationships, of earning some income, and of campaigning for office combined to place a distinct strain on candidates. Campaigning appeared to be very hard work, whether ringing doorbells or greeting a receiving line, since the candidates were usually striving to establish satisfactory relationships with many different types of people, one right after another.

ing their opponents a chance for a campaign dialogue.[9] Nevertheless, incumbents often met with or spoke to more people during the campaign because they drew larger crowds and were allowed to speak at more affairs than nonincumbents. Incumbents also had the advantage of off-year campaigning. Hard-working candidates met or gave speeches to averages of up to 1000 people per week, for a total of up to 15,000 during the campaign. After the election was over, public interest in unsuccessful nonincumbents was virtually nonexistent, but successful incumbents continued to give speeches. For example, one congressman spoke to an average of 800 people per week between the election and the beginning of the next congressional session, a rate which would probably allow him to meet or speak to 15,000 of his constituents beween campaigns. Another congressman commented that the between-campaign speeches were especially valuable because voters thought of congressmen as statesmen between campaigns but as politicians during the campaign.

Incumbents had the advantage of between-campaign mailings. No candidate mailed more than 300,000 pieces of literature during the general election campaign, and the average candidate mailed only 100,000 pieces, but a number of Bay Area congressmen regularly mailed 100,000 to 700,000 pieces of literature each year, including end-of-session reports and questionnaires, both of which are properly regarded as campaign devices.[10] Some of the most effective con-

[9]Incumbents who felt it desirable to campaign were able to leave Congress for various short periods of time as indicated by the activities of the two competitive incumbents. The following comment about that congressional session from *The Reporter*, October 25, 1962, p. 16, is appropriate.

" . . . the legislators appeared to be discovering certain advantages in the unusual length of the session. It was first and foremost an excuse not to debate their campaign opponents. Beyond that, it made their opponents seem just a little unfair to be attacking a man who was off in Washington doing his level best to conduct the nation's business."

[10]The average congressman sent 450,000 pieces of franked mail in fiscal year 1966. U.S. House of Representatives, Committee on Appropriations, Subcommittee on Legislative Branch Appropriations, Ninetieth Congress, First Session, *Hearings on Legislative Branch Appropriations for 1968*, Government Printing Office, Washington, D.C., 1967, p. 372.

gressional mailings, judged by comments made by housewives at coffees, were the infant care books sent to new mothers, and the small Department of Agriculture cookbooks sent to new brides. A note on the wall in one congressional office stated that 1000 copies of these booklets had been mailed in June 1962, indicating a rate of 10,000 or more each year.

Finally, incumbents had the advantage of experience. As the Stimson Bullitt quote at the beginning of the chapter suggests, most candidates tried a little bit of everything. The reasons appeared to be quite different however for experienced and inexperienced candidates. Experienced candidates or managers planned 2 or 3 projects — a get-out-the-vote drive, a major mailing, 500 lawn signs — and carried them off successfully. Minor projects — buttons, bumper stickers, ads in a chamber of commerce program — were agreed to as a means of keeping campaign workers happy, but the costs and efforts were kept to a minimum.

Inexperienced candidates tried everything because they were not sure what would work. They lacked the discipline to restrict themselves to two or three projects, and many of them lacked the resources to carry out any major project. For example, one nonincumbent kept laying out newspaper ads that he was going to run if some money came in. None of the ads were run. Part of the reason for the differences in discipline was that incumbents had the advantage of following the procedures of the last election. One or two major changes might be made but, for the most part, incumbents were able to avoid acrimonious debate among their advisors about the value of projects, as well as the extensive explanations and training of people to carry out projects.

SUMMARY

For one reason and another, candidates believed that they needed to engage in several types of activities, but the emphasis varied from one type of candidate to another. Democrats had to place more emphasis on direct and personal contact with their voters, while Republicans were able to contact their voters by such impersonal means as newspaper advertisements. Because personal contact was especially effective, candidates who wished to be competitive emphasized it. Because it was psychologically difficult, candidates who were sure winners avoided it, if possible. This difference gave incumbents an advantage over their challengers, because challengers had to contact voters to change their normal voting pattern. Incumbents also had the advantage of between-campaign mailings, which were twice as extensive as the campaign mailings of any candidate, and of between-campaign speeches, which were probably more valuable than campaign speeches.

Chapter 9

USE OF RESOURCES — APPEALS

The arguments or appeals that campaigners may use are restricted by the circumstances of their campaigns. Studies of the appeals used in Presidential campaigns usually report that the incumbent or candidate of the in-party defends the government's record while the challenger attacks it. (Harry Truman reversed this somewhat in 1948 by attacking the record of the Republican 80th Congress.) Democrats, being the majority party, urge voters to emphasize party in their vote decisions while Republicans urge a vote for the man, not the party. Democrats urge consideration of domestic issues and especially economic issues, recalling that Republicans were in power at the beginning of the Great Depression. Republicans emphasize foreign policy issues, pointing out that Democrats were in power at the beginning of World War I, World War II, and the Korean War. Each party usually makes some appeals to particular groups, Republicans arguing, for example, that they will help business, Democrats arguing that they will help the working man.[1]

The appeals that Bay Area congressional candidates made were classified by resource, based on their emphasis on the qualities of the candidate, the party, issues, or groups. Analyses were made of materials presented in brochures, newspaper advertisements, speeches, billboards, lawn signs, and

[1] For general discussions of appeals, see V. O. Key, Jr., *Politics, Parties and Pressure Groups*, fifth edition, Thomas Y. Crowell Co., 1964, pp. 462–475; and Nelson W. Polsby and Aaron B. Wildavsky, *Presidential Elections: Strategies of American Electoral Politics*, headline edition, Charles Scribner's Sons, New York, 1964, pp. 94–109.

television advertisements,[2] giving some consideration to the size of the audience in each case. These analyses indicated that probably more than half of the appeals, to the extent that it is possible to speak of proportions in such a multifaceted inexact evaluation, were based on the qualities of the candidate or his opponent. The next largest number of appeals were based on party affiliation, followed by issues and groups. To some extent, however, the appeals that were used depended upon the resources available. For example, one party official, looking over the rather insignificant record of public achievements held by his nonincumbent candidate, advised the candidate to concentrate on the issues rather than to talk about himself. The appeals also depended upon the audience available; some groups of voters were quite interested in issues, while others were more concerned with the party affiliation of the candidates. The number of appeals that were made depended upon the competitiveness of the race, with competitive candidates making many more appeals and types of appeals than either sure winners or sure losers.

Candidate

Much of the advertising by Bay Area congressional candidates emphasized the name and picture of the candidate. This emphasis was needed because surveys have shown that nationally less than one half of the people can identify their congressman, much less his opponent.[3] Incumbents were much less likely than nonincumbents to include other personal information. Nonincumbents presented extensive personal information, including pictures with their families, but incumbents concentrated on their congressional record, as if life had begun after their first election. Only one of the

---

[2]An important group of appeals—those spread individually by word of mouth—were rarely heard and thus could not be evaluated.
[3]Donald E. Stokes and Warren E. Miller, "Party Government and the Salience of Congress," *Public Opinion Quarterly*, 26, 540 (Winter 1962). In their 1958 sample, 39 percent of the respondents said they knew something about the incumbent, whereas 20 percent knew something about the challenger. See also Hadley Cantril, ed., *Public Opinion 1935-1946*, Princeton University Press, Princeton, 1951, p. 133.

eight incumbents used a picture with his family, and this was the most junior of the congressmen. It was not difficult, however, to learn about the background of incumbents. Most of them prepared a fairly complete mimeographed statement about their precongressional backgrounds, and this statement could be picked up by anyone who went to campaign headquarters.

Much of the reason that incumbents presented less personal information was that they had a public service record to speak about. Incumbents emphasized their seniority and experience, a rational emphasis in view of the previously reported findings that voters consider experience more important than any other candidate characteristic. Seniority was argued no matter what the length of time served. One congressman had used this appeal when he was running for his second term. Challengers tried to counteract this argument by asserting, if they could, that the incumbent was too old or that the seniority system was bad.

Incumbents also emphasized their effectiveness, listing the government projects that they had secured for their district. Challengers responded by arguing that the credit really belonged to other congressmen, including predecessors of the incumbent, or that the project would have been secured earlier if someone else had been in office. One challenger publicized the fact that his opponent had not sponsored a single successful bill in 10 years in Congress. (The congressman, a Republican, replied by noting that minority leader Charles Halleck had not sponsored a single successful bill in 25 years in Congress, an argument that, even if true, did not really seem germane to the question of this congressman's effectiveness.) In another case, Congressman William Mailliard cited his fight to preserve the 6 percent differential allowed West Coast shipbuilders as an example of his vigorous representation of San Francisco. His opponent responded by noting that Congress nevertheless had eliminated the differential, indicating that vigor was not the same as effectiveness.

Some congressmen appealed for votes on the basis of their style of representation. One congressman pointed proudly to his record of not having missed a single roll-call vote since entering Congress, so that his district knew where he stood. Another emphasized that he kept in touch with his constituents through his newsletters and congressional polls. Nonincumbents could appeal only on the basis of what they would do. One promised to establish a bipartisan advisory board if elected. Another, Republican L. V. "Mike" Honsinger, said that he would always vote as the people wanted, an argument which was publicly ridiculed by a Democratic congressman from a neighboring district. The congressman argued that legislators must make up their own minds — otherwise they would need to take a public opinion poll on every proposed measure and amendment. (Although this was the clearest case, some other comments indicated that experienced candidates were more likely to emphasize the Burkean notion of an independent trusteeship, while inexperienced candidates thought of a congressman's proper role as that of an instructed delegate.)

The main difference noted between Democrats and Republicans was that Democrats were more likely than Republicans to use family pictures, possibly because family pictures may be more effective with the poorly educated Democratic voters than with the more highly educated Republicans. Such a hypothesis was suggested by the comment of a campaign worker that a brochure devoted entirely to her candidate's family life was especially effective in the heavily Democratic Negro areas of the district.

Party

Public endorsements from Democratic party leaders were usually more valuable than those from Republican party leaders because voters registered as Democrats constituted a majority in almost every district. Republican incumbents who had received endorsements from Democratic leaders or letters of commendation from Democratic congressmen used these materials in appeals to Democratic voters. Democratic challengers replied that they were actually the candidates who were supported by the Democratic party. To prove it, they emphasized their relations with President Kennedy, publicizing their pictures with him, letters from him, and their own promises to support him. Appeals based upon a connection with the Republican party were rarely made by Republican candidates except in material directed specifically to Republican voters. (One candidate used pictures of himself with Barry Goldwater and liberal Republican Senator Thomas Kuchel in his mailings to Republicans, but dropped the Goldwater picture in the brochure for Democrats.) Democratic candidates, of course, tried to make sure that Democratic voters knew that their opponents were Republican.

Issues

The Cuba missile crisis occurred about two weeks before the election, making Cuba the most important issue in the campaign. Two or three Republican congressmen had been publicly calling for more aggressive action by the United States, and their Democratic opponents had charged them with "jingoism." When President Kennedy demanded the ouster of Russian missiles, most candidates publicly supported his action, but the Republican congressmen were able to say "I told you so," and the Democratic challengers felt that any hope of electoral victory had been lost. "Peace" was a fairly important issue in at least three Democratic primary election campaigns, but its significance faded as the summer wore on and the Cuba missile crisis doomed the hopes of peace-oriented candidates.

Except for Cuba, the emphasis was on domestic issues.[4] Two issues—medicare and civil rights—were discussed by candidates of both parties. Generally, Democrats favored medicare and Republicans opposed it, occasionally proposing instead reliance on the Kerr-Mills program or on a volun-

[4]The issues that were emphasized in the campaigns correlated to some extent with the differences in party views expressed in the campaign workers survey. Out of the nine issues listed, the greatest divisions in views between workers for Republican and Democratic candidates, were about the issues of (1) federal action to increase employment, (2) federal programs of medical care for the aged, and (3) federal aid to education. Foreign policy issues resulted in the least division between workers for each party.

tary medical care program. Candidates of both parties supported civil rights measures, but the amount of emphasis depended upon the percentage of Negroes in the district and the personal attitudes of the candidates. Otherwise Democratic candidates discussed the United Nations bond proposal, urban problems, trade expansion, full employment, tax reform, and aid to education, while Republicans placed emphasis on opposition to heavy government spending programs, support of local government, and support of constitutional government. As the reader will note, the issues emphasized by Democrats were more specific than those emphasized by Republicans.

Several attempts were made to pin opponents with unpopular views, usually by indicating that the opponent was overly liberal or overly conservative. For example, two challengers compared the voting records of Congressman John Rousselot, a member of the John Birch Society, with the voting records of the Republican incumbents they were challenging, noting the similarities.[5] A Republican challenger talked about his opponent's 100 percent support of issues considered important by the Americans for Democratic Action, and John O'Connell's opponent noted that as an Assemblyman, O'Connell had opposed a pledge-to-the-flag bill, which had been supported by a large majority of the legislators and signed by the governor.

In their appeals based on issues, incumbents discussed bills they had sponsored or issues already before Congress, while nonincumbents often discussed future legislation. Competitive candidates advertised their views on more issues than did sure winners and sure losers, although some sure losers who tried hard to be competitive presented numerous issue views.

[5]Some Democrats considered this just retribution for Richard Nixon's use of the technique against Helen Gahagan Douglas in 1950, when he had compared her record to that of left-wing Congressman Vito Marcantonio. Such comparisons are usually specious because many congressional votes are nearly unanimous. Thus Nixon frequently voted with Marcantonio also, and the 1962 challengers, if they had been in Congress, would have probably voted with Rousselot a seemingly high percentage of the time.

Groups

Comparatively few appeals were based on the support a candidate had from groups or the support he gave to a group's cause. The most common types of appeals in this category were statements that the candidate had support from labor unions, aged people, newspapers, or local government officials. Competitive candidates, who made more appeals of all types than noncompetitive candidates, made more group appeals also. Democrats made more group appeals than Republicans, but most of the difference was in their statements indicating that they had been endorsed by labor unions. Incumbents and state legislators had the advantage of being able to give the impression of group support by reprinting thank-you letters sent by organizations that they had helped. Occasionally challengers retaliated by pointing out that incumbents had also helped other groups, which did not have such high public esteem, such as downtown merchants or the drug lobby.

Unfair Appeals

Most Bay Area candidates had few complaints about the campaign tactics of their opponents, but there were some questionable practices — a last minute letter in one campaign, unfounded rumors about the sex life of a candidate in another, and a false charge that an incumbent had left a congressional session early to take a Caribbean cruise. The cases available, though limited in number, indicated that in this geographical area the large majority of unfair campaign practices were perpetrated by people inexperienced in politics. The most obvious difference was between incumbents and nonincumbents. Incumbents had participated in an extensive socialization process in Congress, a process which required that a politician be polite and fairly straightforward with his opponents, recognizing that the game of politics could continue only if kept within certain bounds. Today's opponent might be tomorrow's ally, if he was not permanently alienated by personal charges. This attitude was carried over into political campaigns and incumbents appeared to be less likely to engage in unfair practices than nonincumbents.[6] There was some correlation between competitiveness and unfairness, however, with sure winners having nothing to gain by being unfair, with competitive candidates having an office to gain, and with sure losers occasionally becoming convinced that they could become competitive only by sharp attacks on the opposition.

SUMMARY

More than half of the appeals made to voters were based on the characteristics or name identification of the candidates. Party, issues, and groups followed in order, although the distribution depended to some extent on the resources and audience available. Incumbents had several advantages over nonincumbents. Discussions of experience, effectiveness, style of representation, and issue positions tended to revolve around the incumbent's record. In addition, incumbents, especially Republican incumbents, could make more effective appeals to voters of the opposite party because they were more likely than nonincumbents to have support from leaders of that party. Incumbents could also make more effective appeals to groups or group sympathizers because they were more likely to have endorsements or seeming endorsements from the groups. The principal difference between Republicans and Democrats was the issues they emphasized and the use of family pictures, which apparently were judged to be more effective in appeals to Democratic than Republican voters. The principal difference between competitive and noncompetitive candidates was in the volume of appeals, with competitive candidates making many more appeals of all types, including issue appeals. The number of unfair appeals was limited, and came mostly from inexperienced campaigners.

[6] In a number of cases, incumbents and their previous opponents had a warm and continuing friendship. Three such former opponents supported Congressman Mailliard in 1962. In another district, the challenger came to have such high respect for his incumbent-opponent that he dropped some charges at the incumbent's request and promised to support him in his next campaign (which was for a nonpartisan office rather than for reelection).

Chapter 10

IMPLICATIONS FOR DEMOCRACY

Competition is by definition, particularly the definitions adopted for this study, vital for democracy. As Joseph Schumpeter has said, the right to make political decisions is acquired "by means of a *competitive* struggle for the people's vote."[1] The importance of competition is further indicated by the empirical findings of this study, especially when these findings are converted into indicators of political participation, a cornerstone of democracy.

By almost any measure—financial contributions, campaign work, receipt of literature, or voting—residents of competitive districts were more likely to participate than residents of noncompetitive districts. The average number of financial contributors was more than twice as high in competitive as in noncompetitive districts. Three times as many people worked in congressional campaigns in competitive districts, and the increased need for campaign workers allowed and encouraged more women and more low-income people to participate in politics. The average voter in competitive districts received twice as many pieces of mail, and was the target of 20 times as much television and radio advertising, twice as much billboard and sign advertising, and half again as much newspaper advertising, judged by expenditures. According to reports of campaign worker activities, voters in competitive districts were 3 or 4 times as likely as voters in noncompetitive districts to receive a telephone call or a visit from a campaign worker. They were also more likely to be

---

[1] Joseph A. Schumpeter, *Capitalism, Socialism and Democracy*, third edition, Harper and Row, New York, 1962, p. 269. (Emphasis added.)

Implications for Democracy 121

visited by one or both candidates, judged by the finding that competitive candidates averaged 150 days campaigning, compared to 50 for noncompetitive candidates.

A frequent response to such findings is that, while competitive candidates may campaign and advertise more, the need to be competitive means that their advertisements, mailings, and speeches will contain less information about government and contemporary problems because they will not want to alienate voters by being specific.[2] The evidence indicates that the reverse was true in these ten districts, with competitive candidates presenting more information on more issues than noncompetitive candidates. Even among noncompetitive candidates, the most extensive presentations of information were by the sure losers who were trying hard to be competitive.

Increased participation was also indicated by the voting rate. In 1962 votes were cast by 81.5 percent of the registered voters in the competitive Bay Area districts, and by 77.7 percent of the registered voters in noncompetitive districts.[3] These figures indicate that, even though many voters do not know the name of their congressman, competitive congressional campaigns will apparently increase voter turnout by about 4 percentage points over that for districts with noncompetitive campaigns. The increase in turnout can be attributed generally to the increased stimulation—the advertisements, the pieces of mail, the telephone calls from workers—and specifically to the fact that more than 800 campaign workers for congressional candidates were active in getting out the

[2] Hugh Bone presents such a view in *American Politics and the Party System*, third edition, McGraw-Hill, New York, 1965, p. 401. "Candidates who come from a safe district or who are thoroughly entrenched and assured of winning often take a specific stand on certain issues which could not be taken in a close contest. At the other extreme, third-party candidates and the Republican or Democrat hopelessly in the minority can afford to be specific and make definite promises."
[3] This is total vote cast, not vote for congressional candidates, which was about 6 percentage points lower due to drop-off. The difference between competitive and noncompetitive districts is probably not due to socioeconomic characteristics of the constituencies, because constructed medians indicated that the educational levels in the two types of districts were similar and the income levels were higher in the noncompetitive districts.

vote on election day in the average competitive district compared to 250 in the average noncompetitive district.

Unfortunately, given the importance of competition, only 3 of the 10 districts were competitive in the congressional races, although 4 more might well have been, considering that those 4 voted in 1962 for both Democrat Pat Brown for Governor and Republican Thomas Kuchel for Senator. Even in the remaining 3, both Brown and Kuchel had at least 48 percent of the vote. This lack of competitiveness, in contrast to the potential, poses a serious problem for democracy.

Ordinarily the political parties are thought of as the agents for competition. States or districts are regularly labeled by such terms as two-party, weak two-party and one-party, or by such terms as safe Democratic or leaning Republican. The comparison of primary elections (when parties are not creating competition) with general elections (when they are) clearly shows that the parties greatly increase the amount of competition in the United States. The examination of the results in Bay Area elections suggests that, even so, they are not strong enough to make competitive even half of the potentially competitive districts.

The remaining districts were not competitive because of the significant advantage held by incumbents, no matter what their party, over nonincumbents. In the acquisition of each and every resource, incumbents, as a rule, were able to acquire it more easily. For nonincumbents the acquisition of resources was one long series of requests and pleas. Some candidates found it embarrassing or difficult to continually ask relatives to give more of their savings, to ask friends to spend their Sundays ringing doorbells, and to ask acquaintances to withdraw their publicly announced support for an opponent. One reason was that the requests of nonincumbents were much more likely to be denied than the requests of incumbents. Another was that the requests which were granted would likely have to be repaid in the local community. Such a possibility was clearly noted by one candidate who said that if he lost, he and his wife would be prime targets for every civic affair and charity drive in town for years to come.[4] Such repayment requirements meant that many candidates could expect that it would take several years to repay the financial and social debts incurred in their campaigns, a specter which caused some nonincumbents to reduce the number of requests for resources.

In the distribution of campaign resources, incumbents had the advantage of previous experience. One incumbent, when informed by his campaign workers that the challenger was conducting a daily radio program, responded by saying, "That's all right. We tried that before and found that nobody in this district listened, so let him go ahead and try it." Later the challenger came to the same conclusion. Another challenger did not realize until late in the campaign that the small groups before which he appeared were impressed by him but the large groups were not, indicating that he should spend his time only with small groups. One inexperienced candidate inappropriately concluded that he could win more votes by concentrating on precincts dominated by the opposite party rather than his own, only to find on election day that he lost votes he should have won from his own party and failed to convert any perceptible number of opponents. The challenger in one wealthy district studied hard on welfare and labor issues before making his appeal to labor unions, only to find that local union members already had advantageous labor contracts, and were concerned mostly about hunting, fishing, and recreational resources. This wastage of resources and making of inappropriate appeals meant that nonincumbents did not use even the resources they had as efficiently as incumbents did.

A particular case study—the campaign in the Fourteenth District, an industrial and suburban East Bay district—may help to illustrate the advantages of the incumbent. More than 60 percent of the district's voters were registered as Democrats and all three of the state legislators from the district were Democrats. However, the incumbent congressman, John Baldwin, was a Republican, indicating that this was

[4]Fortunately he won and was able to move to Washington, D.C., with the other incumbents, free from many of these repayment obligations.

a district that the Democratic candidate should easily have made competitive.

In this situation, the resource most needed for a competitive campaign was an attractive candidate. None of the state legislators in the district wished to run against Baldwin,[5] so they met to recruit or select a candidate. One of them had been approached earlier by Charles Weidner who had expressed interest in doing campaign work as a means of gaining experience before running for office himself. Weidner mentioned an interest in Congress, and the legislator replied that he would need to be much better known to have a chance of winning in the district. Nevertheless, the legislators decided to ask Weidner to run, promising him their support. Weidner consented after consulting with CDC and labor union officials, both of whom encouraged him. He started with an immediate disadvantage, having never held office nor run before. Nor was he well known in the district, having moved there only five years before, and having located his business, a health and welfare pension consulting firm, outside the district. He was, however, personable, well liked, respected by those who knew him, and intelligent.

Given Weidner's inexperience and comparative anonymity, the prospects of success were limited without substantial financial resources. Weidner was willing to contribute several thousand dollars as well as his time and personal expenses, but he did not possess the personal contribution of $40,000 or more that would have been needed to free the campaign from financial problems. Furthermore, the Fourteenth was not a wealthy district, so that money was difficult to raise. Weidner utilized various proven and imaginative techniques, such as appointing the 1960 Democratic candidate as campaign treasurer and holding a pledge breakfast to which potential contributors were invited. (About half of those who pledged contributions actually made them.) These procedures resulted in a campaign chest of about $18,000,

---

[5]Baldwin died in 1966, and one of the state legislators successfully ran for the seat, indicating that he may well have been interested in Congress in 1962, but did not wish to challenge Baldwin. In such a situation, a potential candidate would not necessarily want to recruit a likely winner.

including Weidner's personal contribution, a significant figure but woefully short of that which was needed.

Given the comparative value of the candidate and financial resources, Weidner could hope to win only with wholehearted party support, a large number of workers, some issue advantage, and some group support. In most cases he was doomed to failure. A maverick Democrat filed against Weidner in the primary, forcing him into use of some of his limited financial resources. His narrow win over the maverick indicated that he had limited vote-getting ability so that other resources were thereafter more difficult to acquire. Baldwin also contributed to Weidner's primary election problems by sending a brochure to all Democrats, successfully asking for a large write-in vote in the Democratic primary, a technique that goes back to the days of cross-filing. The efforts to recruit campaign workers were extensive but not particularly successful. The first campaign manager, a volunteer, resigned, and the second, who was hired, proved unsatisfactory and left. A weekly bulletin designed to recruit workers was sent to about 1000 CDC members and past Democratic workers, but only about 100 people worked in Weidner's campaign. (Those people contributed wholeheartedly, one schoolteacher passing up a $3000 summer job in order to work as a volunteer for Weidner.) The efforts to acquire issue information were extensive and successful. Weidner took trips to Washington, D.C., at his own expense, consulted with his brother, Edward Weidner, a well-known political scientist, hired a research firm, and studied hard. He had the misfortune, however, to be running against one of the best-informed of the Bay Area congressman, and audiences who listened to their debates were continually impressed with the extensive and fantastically detailed knowledge possessed by Baldwin. Similarly, Weidner had strong (but not unanimous) support from labor unions, but had difficulty securing support from other groups because he was running against a well-liked opponent who had for years sent congratulatory letters to newly elected officers of all sorts of groups, offering them the services of his office.

In summary, despite an $18,000 campaign fund, a 60 percent Democratic district, and the support of labor unions and 100 workers, despite being personable, well-informed, and willing to campaign for 100 days and contribute extensively to his own campaign, Weidner was able to win only 37 percent of the vote. His opponent spent only $8300 and campaigned for less than 20 days. Some of Baldwin's advantages were personal—he was widely respected by many Democrats as well as Republicans—but other advantages were those of any incumbent, for example, a field secretary who served as campaign manager, a salary while campaigning, and the franking privilege for his annual poll.

Lest the general findings and this case study present too sharp a picture, some qualifications should be noted. First the advantages of incumbency, while applicable to most office holders, are more applicable to congressmen than to most others. Across the nation, in presidential election years from 1924 to 1956, 88 percent of all incumbent congressmen ran for reelection and 90 percent of these candidates were reelected, resulting in the return of 79 percent of the incumbents. The percentages, high as they are, have been steadily inching upwards.[6] These figures may be contrasted with the 1946–1964 record of previously elected Senators, and the 1960–1964 record of members of the Missouri House of Representatives, two examples of incumbents in other offices who have not been as successful as congressmen, as shown in Table 1.[7]

In addition, the advantages of incumbents in California are apparently greater than the advantages of incumbents elsewhere. In the United States the median incumbent congressman running for reelection in 1960 ran about 4 percentage points ahead of his party's presidential candidate, while

[6]Milton Cummings, "Congressmen and the Electorate: A Study of House Elections in Presidential Years, 1920–1956," unpublished Ph.D. thesis, Harvard University, Cambridge, 1960, pp. 129, 133. The figures are approximate because complete figures are not available for the early years.
[7]Compiled from Congressional Quarterly, *Politics in America, 1945–64*, Congressional Quarterly, Washington, D.C., 1965, pp. 100–109; and from *Official Manuals, State of Missouri*, Secretary of State, Jefferson City, Missouri. One reason why the proportion of Senators who ran for reelection is low is that a comparatively high proportion of Senators died before the completion of their 6-year term.

TABLE 1
Reelection Record of Incumbent Officeholders

	U. S. Representatives (1924-56)	U. S. Senators (1946-64)	Missouri Representatives (1960-64)
Percent who ran for reelection	88	76	85
Percent of those who ran who were successful	90	79	73
Percent of incumbents returned to office	79	60	62

Source. See text, Footnote 7.

in California the median incumbent congressman ran about 8 percentage points ahead of his party's presidential candidate. The comparable percentages for 1964 were 4 and 5.[8] One reason for this is that California law allows candidates to list their occupation on the ballot so that voters are told who is the incumbent. The law also requires that incumbents be listed first on the ballot, which provides a slight advantage. The partisan independence of California voters, compared to voters of other states, would also contribute to increased ticket splitting, and thus frequently to a greater advantage for incumbents.

Finally, one special factor—the Cuba missile crisis—may have been of importance in 1962. The crisis, which threatened the entire country with the possibility of nuclear destruction, came only two weeks before the election, and the reaction of voters may well have been to hesitate before changing leadership at such a critical point. Such hesitation was indicated by the fact that the number of United States congressmen defeated in the general election in 1962 was

[8]Based on compilations from Congressional Quarterly, *Politics in America, 1945-64*, Ibid., pp. 118-123; *Congressional Quarterly Almanac, 1963*, Congressional Quarterly, Washington, D.C., 1963, pp. 1163-1168; and California Secretary of State, *Statement of Vote: General Election and Special Elections in the 11th, 38th and 79th Assembly Districts, November 8, 1960*, California State Printing Office, Sacramento, 1960.

slightly below normal, despite the addition of some defeats caused by reapportionment plans which placed two incumbents into the same district or provided incumbents with districts designed to cause their defeat.

These qualifications indicate that campaign studies conducted in other areas, concerned with other offices, observing the campaigns in different years, might reach other conclusions. Studies of primary elections would probably indicate even greater advantages for incumbents because of the need for personal resources, while studies of presidential-year elections might indicate less advantage because of the greater resources available to all candidates in those election years. Studies of less compact districts would probably find greater emphasis on the localism of the candidate, a pattern which was indicated in the Bay Area, comparing the two large districts with the eight more compact districts. Nevertheless, each study would probably find distinct advantages for incumbents, especially congressional incumbents. These advantages are so significant, not only in California but all across the nation, that they pose questions for the citizens of democracy.

To what extent is meaningful and substantial competition essential for a democracy? Are democratic processes sufficiently safeguarded merely by the nomination of a candidate from the opposite party, although his probabilities of success are low? Meaningful competition does not necessarily mean a close race every 2 years; the U.S. Senate appears democratic despite its 6-year term. The 2-year congressional term may, in fact, reduce the amount of competition because it means that the minority party has to present some sacrificial candidate every biennium. Because of the voracious appetite of the 2-year term, some minority parties are probably forced into presenting potential candidates before they are ready, just as Weidner was persuaded to run before he had campaign experience or was well known. However, meaningful competition should mean a close race now and then. One Bay Area district has not had a close race in either the primary or general election since 1944. The lack of competition is a tribute to the district's congressman, but it also means that many district voters have never been confronted forcefully and meaningfully with alternative policies, or alternative personalities. Meaningful competition does not require electoral contests for every office, either. Within our system, such contests are not conducted for Supreme Court Judgeships or cabinet positions. At some point, however, the elimination of competition endangers democracy. Most people would consider democracy weakened if the House of Representatives were to be appointed by the President, as is the Supreme Court. Some thought does need to be given then to the minimum level of competition needed for congressional seats. The question is relevant for consideration of those proposals that further increase the advantages of incumbents, such as increases in staff personnel and mailing privileges.

Although it is a consideration external to the model of democracy employed here, we must also consider the extent to which a high rate of meaningful competition might be harmful to sound government. Congress can operate effectively only if it includes skilled and experienced men, and such men may lose their posts if a majority of districts become competitive. Increasing competition would require more congressmen to raise $50,000 every 2 years, to secure 500 or more campaign workers, to spend many days campaigning, to bid for the support of nonpolitical groups, and to concentrate on relationships with their constituencies. These activities would reduce the amount of time that they could dedicate to solving national problems. The certainty of increased competition might also result in different types of people entering political contests; we do not know whether these people would be as suited for the tasks of Congress as present congressmen. On the other hand, Congress should be responsive to the public, and the findings of this study demonstrate that candidates in noncompetitive districts make fewer efforts than candidates in competitive districts to learn the views of the public.

These questions will have to be answered by the citizens of democracy. The findings from this study indicate that the amount of meaningful competition for Congress is, contrary

130   Implications for Democracy

to popular belief, fairly limited. Opinions may vary however as to whether the return of about 80 percent of all incumbents, as in the case of Congressman, or about 60 percent, as in the case of Senators and legislators, or some other figure, is appropriate. For those who believe that the present amount of competition or even less is appropriate, there is little need for concern; congressmen have proved themselves adept at acquiring and exploiting campaign advantages. Those who would decrease the competition and turnover for other offices, such as state legislatures, need only look as far as Congress for examples. For those who believe that more competition is needed, various policies might be considered.

The policies are suggested especially by the factors in those congressional elections in which incumbents have been defeated. The number of defeated incumbents varies from year to year, indicating that national trends have significant effects. For example, 1958 was a Democratic year and many Republicans lost their seats, including one from the Bay Area. Some congressmen lose their seats after each decennial reapportionment, in some cases because state legislatures have drawn districts intended to bring about their defeat. Congressman William Mailliard was able to defeat an incumbent after the Republican reapportionment of 1951, and Democrats had hoped to return the favor when they reapportioned in 1961. In some cases, congressmen lose because their challengers possess greater resources than they do. The voluntary retirements in recent years of two Bay Area congressmen appear to have been related to the substantial campaign resources possessed by potential challengers. In both cases the challengers had demonstrated their vote-getting ability; one challenger was helped by substantial personal funds, and the other had built an effective and loyal personal organization. Finally, some congressmen lose their seats because of personal errors or problems, including advocating policies that differ from widely and strongly held views of district voters. As an example of a personal problem, Robert Condon lost his congressional seat to John Baldwin in 1954, after he had been barred on security grounds from witnessing an atomic test. Frequently recurring personal problems are ill health and old age. In many cases, the defeat of an incumbent requires a combination of factors. Baldwin had previously been defeated by Condon, just as Mailliard had been previously defeated by the incumbent he replaced in 1952, indicating that their personal resources were not sufficient but had to be combined with other factors.

The effect of reapportionment suggests the policy of the prevention of gerrymandering — the drawing of districts in order to give an advantage or disadvantage to one particular group. The natural tendency of district architects is to make a district safe for one particular party or individual, rather than to insure continued competitiveness. The frequently expressed but infrequently followed criteria of compactness for legislative districts is designed to reduce gerrymandering. A substitution of the concept of competitiveness for compactness would provide a much more explicit statement of the goal and would allow clearer and easier measures of whether the goal had been accomplished. The adoption of such a criteria, while it would increase competitiveness, would not, this study has shown, insure it, because the advantages of incumbents are often sufficient to overcome normal expectations of competitiveness.

Other policies, which the citizen of democracy might well want to consider, would relate to the acquisition and use of campaign resources, especially for nonincumbents. The federal government subsidizes the campaigns of incumbents but not of challengers. The government contributes congressional salaries during the campaign, salaries of field representatives who are serving as campaign managers, franking privileges which allow congressmen to poll constituents or send thinly veiled campaign literature at limited cost, extensive research facilities such as the Library of Congress, free office space (which may obviate need for renting a campaign headquarters), and secretarial staff. Such advantages are probably worth at least $25,000 per campaign for each incumbent, thus representing a $25,000 deficit with which each challenger is immediately faced. Proponents of governmental campaign subsidies might well consider equalizing these advantages by extending the franking privilege and opening

Library of Congress facilities to challengers, and by providing financing for the hiring of campaign managers and secretarial staff, and for office space. Proponents might even consider the radical proposal of paying a salary to major party nominees, since the challengers are making a substantial contribution to a democratic system by presenting competition. At present those few individuals who become candidates are expected to contribute disproportionately out of their own pockets to the operation of democracy. If he contributes extensively to the operation of democracy, the challenger is a public servant. Some, but not all, public servants are compensated by the government for their activities. An alternative, already practiced in several Bay Area districts, is campaign salary payments to candidates and campaign managers by industrial companies and interest groups.

Competition might be increased by strengthening the political parties. Financial contributions to the party hierarchy might not always be effective — some candidates noted that county central committees spent their funds to buttress their own power rather than to assist candidates. A party victory would have upset the power structure, according to these candidates. However, the establishment of precinct organizations relieved candidates of the necessity of recruiting large numbers of campaign workers. Furthermore, the campaign schools conducted by national party committees were quite helpful to new candidates, and might be extended. Since candidates had to pay their own expenses, some of the candidates who most needed the assistance were unable to attend. Party organizations might also provide more issue information earlier. After his defeat, Charles Weidner formed a political club designed to gather information about issues before Congress and the policies of Congressman Baldwin. These data were to be presented to the district's next challenger, so that he would not need to spend as much time studying as Weidner had spent. Hopefully the challenger might even have been a member of the club, acquainting himself with the issues over a two-year period.

Some other aspects of American political culture and law reduce the number of potential candidates available. The

waste of, 76
national committees, contributions from, 41
out-of-district contributors, 83
personal contacts, responses from audiences, 51
primary elections, 38
professional public opinion polls, use of, 54
recontributions, 81
search for information on content of issues, 56–58
style of representation, 115
timeliness of contributions, 76
unfair appeals, 118
use of procedures from previous campaign, 110
voters, number met, 109
workers, attitudes of, toward candidates, 95
  characteristics of, 93
  number of, 91
  political attitudes of, 95, 96
  replacement of, 98
  sources of, 92–93
Incumbents, advantages of, 122–128
  competition in primary and general elections, 34
Independent Progressives, 8
Indiana, 24
Industrial companies, 18, 132
Inexperienced candidates, see Candidates, inexperienced
Infant care books, 110
Interest groups, see Groups
Inter-university Consortium for Political Research, see Survey Research Center, University of Michigan
Issue advisory committees, 58
Issues, 48–60
  appeals based on, 116
  clubs to study, 132
  determining voter opinions on, 48–55
  in Fourteenth District, 125
  importance as a campaign resource, in general elections, 14
  in primary elections, 33
  search for information on content of, 55–59

Janowitz, Morris, 86
Javits, Jacob, 52
John Birch Society, 7, 64, 117
Johnson, Hiram, 6, 7, 8
Johnson, Lyndon, 133
Judah, Charles B., 19, 20, 21

Katz, Daniel, 86
Keller, William, 136
Kelley, Stanley, 87
Kennedy, John F., 11, 13, 26, 40, 42, 45, 115, 116
Kessel, John H., 49
Key, V. O., Jr., 3, 33, 112
Kindig, Everett, 87, 100
Knowland, William, 68
Korchin, Sheldon J., 24, 25, 26
Kovac, Frank, 78
Kriesberg, Martin, 49
Kuchel, Thomas, 9, 116, 122

Labor unions, 13, 63, 67, 70, 123, 124
  Bay Area, 67, 68, 70
  see also Committee on Political Education (AFL-CIO)
Ladies Garment Workers Union, International, 63
Landon, Alf, 52
Lane, Robert E., 49, 90
Lazarfeld, Paul F., 64, 103
Leadership ability of candidates, 27
Lee, Eugene C., 9, 64
Leege, David, 24, 64
Leggett, Robert, 11, 17, 40, 44, 45, 97, 135
Legislative Primary Elections in Austin, Texas, 1962, see Olson, David M.
Legislative Reference Service, 56, 59
Legislative System: Explorations in Legislative Behavior, The, see Wahlke, John C.
Legislators, Missouri, reelection success, 126
Lerner, Harry, 87
Letters of endorsement, from Presi-

usual expectation in America is that a candidate will be a resident of the district in which he runs, but this requirement reduces competition because some districts have a larger number of attractive candidates than do other districts. The mobility of California's population has partially eliminated this requirement and, as a result, 3 of the 20 Bay Area candidates did not live in the district in which they were running. Each candidate would have had far less success in the district in which he lived. The prohibition, by custom and law, from running for two offices also restricts competition. Frequently the strongest competition for congressmen comes from state legislators, but usually such men must give up their legislative seat in order to run for Congress. If they were allowed to run for both offices, just as Lyndon Johnson ran for both the U.S. Senate and the Vice-Presidency in 1960, the level of competitiveness in congressional races would probably be increased. Finally, consideration might be given to the British system of nominating a challenger long before the election, and allowing him to serve as the nominee for several elections. Such an extended period of nomination would make clearer his role as a public servant and would allow him more time to become familiar with issues and to become widely known.

Some of these suggestions, especially the suggestion that congressmen vote campaign salaries to their challengers, are not likely to be adopted immediately, but they should be considered by those who wish to increase the competition for congressional seats. As this study has shown, that competition is less formidable than commonly believed, and it is gradually decreasing because incumbents are securing more and more advantages over their challengers.

Appendix A
List of Candidates in Bay Area Congressional Campaigns, 1962

DISTRICT	REPUBLICAN	DEMOCRAT
1. (Competitive)	Donald Clausen, 39, insurance salesman, county supervisor of Del Norte County	*Rep. Clem Miller, 45, killed in plane crash while campaigning
4. (Competitive)	Admiral L. V. (Mike) Honsinger, 57, former commander of shipyard	*Robert Leggett, 36, lawyer, State Assemblyman
5. (One-sided)	Ron Charles, 25, student, part-time accountant	*Rep. John Shelley, 57, former union official, subsequently elected Mayor of San Francisco
6. (Competitive)	*Rep. William Mailliard, 45, former administrator	John O'Connell, 43, lawyer, State Assemblyman
7. (One-sided)	Leonard Cantando, 31, stock broker	*Rep. Jeffery Cohelan, 48, former union official, former Berkeley city councilman
8. (One-sided)	Harold Petersen, 37, school teacher, former Alameda city councilman	*Rep. George P. Miller, 71, chairman of House Committee on Science and Astronautics

DISTRICT	REPUBLICAN	DEMOCRAT
9. (One-sided)	Joseph Donovan, 54, executive secretary to medical society	°W. Donlon Edwards, 47, businessman, subsequently elected national president of Americans for Democratic Action
10. (One-sided)	°Rep. Charles Gubser, 46, former State Assemblyman	James P. Thurber, Jr., 34, Stanford administrator, mayor of Los Altos, distant cousin of the noted humorist
11. (One-sided)	°Rep. Arthur Younger, 69, former real estate financier	William Keller, 34, reporter for *San Francisco Chronicle*
14. (One-sided)	°Rep. John Baldwin, 47, lawyer	Charles Weidner, 43, consultant on health and welfare plans.

°Winner

CLASSIFICATION OF THE CANDIDATES BY PARTY, INCUMBENCY AND COMPETITIVENESS IS AS FOLLOWS:

	Incumbents		Nonincumbents	
	Republicans	Democrats	Republicans	Democrats
Sure Winners	10 – Gubser 11 – Younger 14 – Baldwin	5 – Shelley 7 – Cohelan 8 – G. Miller		9 – Edwards
Competitive Candidates	6 – Mailliard	1 – C. Miller	1 – Clausen 4 – Honsinger	6 – O'Connell 4 – Leggett
Sure losers			5 – Charles 7 – Cantando 8 – Petersen 9 – Donovan	10 – Thurber 11 – Keller 14 – Weidner

The limited number of campaigns and the fact that most of the sure winners were incumbents meant that there were insufficient data to clearly indicate relationships in some cases.

Appendix B
Questionnaire Used in Survey of Campaign Workers

Institute of Governmental Studies   University of California
                                         Berkeley 4, California

CALIFORNIA CONGRESSIONAL CAMPAIGN STUDY

The following questionnaire concerns you and the campaign of your candidate for Congress in 1962. The questions can be answered very quickly with a check mark. Please answer every one. Individual replies will be kept confidential.

1. Were you a personal friend of your Congressional candidate before he announced his candidacy? 4-1[ ] Yes 2[ ] No

2. Did you do any of the following for your candidate in 1962?

                                                    Yes   No

   a. Talk to people to persuade them to vote for
      your candidate . . . . .5-1[ ] 2[ ]
   b. Help register voters . . . . .1[ ] 2[ ]
   c. Help get out the vote on election day . . . . . . .1[ ] 2[ ]
   d. Do door to door canvassing . . . . .1[ ] 2[ ]
   e. Help get out a mailing to voters . . . . 1[ ] 2[ ]
   f. Direct the activities of other campaign
      workers or determine strategy or write up
      campaign materials . . . . 10-1[ ] 2[ ]
   g. Other work you did (please specify) _____
      _____ [ ] [ ]

3. About how many hours did you work for your Congressional candidate?
   13-0[ ] None
        1[ ] 1 to 10 hours
        2[ ] 11 to 20 hours
        3[ ] 21 to 40 hours

138   Appendix B

    4[ ] 41 to 80 hours
    5[ ] 81 to 160 hours
    6[ ] Over 160 hours

4. Please chech each month in 1962 in which you worked for your candidate.
14-1[ ] November   5[ ] July
   2[ ] October   6[ ] June (primary)
   3[ ] September   7[ ] May
   4[ ] August   8[ ] April or before

5. Did you make any kind of financial contribution to his campaign?
    [ ] Yes
15-1[ ] No
If yes, approximately how much?
    2[ ] Less than $5
    3[ ] $5 to $14
    4[ ] $15 to $24
    5[ ] $25 to $99
    6[ ] $100 to $499
    7[ ] $500 or more

6. Had you worked in any election campaigns prior to 1962?
[ ] Yes   1[ ] No
If yes, approximately how many previous campaigns had you worked in?
16-2[ ] One
    3[ ] Two or three
    4[ ] Four or five
    5[ ] Six or more
Had you ever helped before in a campaign for the man who was your 1962 Congressional candidate? 17-1[ ] Yes   2[ ] No

7. What party category do you fit in?
18/   [ ] Republican
     [ ] Democrat
     [ ] Independent
     [ ] Other party
If Republican or Democrat, would you call yourself a strong member of your party or a not very strong member?
    [ ] Strong member
    [ ] Not very strong member

If Independent, do you lean toward the Democrats or Republicans?
[ ] Democrats
[ ] Republicans
[ ] Neither

8. Here is a list of issues about which people often disagree. Please check what you think should be done in each case.

		Should be increased	Should remain as is	Should be decreased
a.	Foreign aid	19–1[ ]	2[ ]	3[ ]
b.	Federal action to increase employment	1[ ]	2[ ]	3[ ]
c.	Restrictions on Communists in the U.S.	1[ ]	2[ ]	3[ ]
d.	Federal programs for medical care for the aged	1[ ]	2[ ]	3[ ]
e.	American participation in the U.N.	1[ ]	2[ ]	3[ ]
f.	Federal aid to education	1[ ]	2[ ]	3[ ]
g.	Military activity against Communist satellites	1[ ]	2[ ]	3[ ]
h.	Federal action to decrease racial discrimination	1[ ]	2[ ]	3[ ]
i.	Nuclear bomb testing	27–1[ ]	2[ ]	3[ ]

9. Political clubs: Do you belong to:
Yes   No
28–1[ ]   [ ] Young Repubs. or Young Demos.
   2[ ]   [ ] A CDC club (Cal. Demo. Council)
   3[ ]   [ ] A Republican Women's club
   4[ ]   [ ] Any other political club

10. What was the last grade you completed in school?
29–1[ ] Some high school or less
   2[ ] High school graduate
   3[ ] Some college
   4[ ] College graduate (B.A. or B.S.)
   5[ ] Some graduate or advanced study
   6[ ] Graduate or advanced professional degree

11. What is your sex?
30–1[ ] Male 2[ ] Female

Appendix B

12. Are you (or the head of your household) employed by the government, either Federal, state or local?
31–1[ ] Yes 2[ ] No

13. Which of the following employment categories do you ordinarily fit in?
32–1[ ] Employed full time
    2[ ] Employed part time
    3[ ] Full time housewife
    4[ ] Retired
    5[ ] Other

14. What is your annual family income?
33–1[ ] Under $8,000
    2[ ] $8,000 to $9,999
    3[ ] $10,000 to $11,999
    4[ ] $12,000 to $14,999
    5[ ] $15,000 to $24,999
    6[ ] $25,000 or more

15. What is your age?
34–1[ ] Under 25 years
    2[ ] 25 to 34 years
    3[ ] 35 to 44 years
    4[ ] 45 to 54 years
    5[ ] 55 to 64 years
    6[ ] 65 years or more

We would appreciate any other comments you wish to make about these questions, your Congressional candidate, his election campaign, or how you got involved in it. You may use the space below and the other side of this sheet if you wish. Thank you very much.

INDEX

Aberbach, Joel D., 63
Acquaintances, number by candidates, 29
Activities, campaign, 100–111
Advertising agencies, 88
AFL-CIO Committee on Political Education, *see* Committee on Political Education
Age of candidates, 28
Alienated Voter, The: Politics in Boston, 24, 25
Amateur workers, *see* Workers, amateur
America Votes 4: A Handbook of Contemporary American Election Statistics, 34
American Civil Liberties Union, 64
American Legion, 63
American Medical Association, 63
American Politics and the Party System, 121
American State Politics: An Introduction, 33
American Voter, The, *see* Campbell, Angus
Americans for Constitutional Action, 62, 64
Americans for Democratic Action, 62, 64, 117, 136
Anderson, Totton J., 9
Appeals, 112–119
classification of, 112
Arizona, *see* Riggs, Robert
Audience reaction to candidates, 51

Babysitting costs, 81
Baldwin, John, 123, 130, 132, 136
Ballot proposition 24, *see* Francis amendment
Banfield, Edward C., 58
Baus and Ross, 87
Bay Area, *see* San Francisco Bay Area
Berelson, Bernard R., 64, 103
Between-campaign speeches and mailings, 109
Bliss, Ray C., 24
Bone, Hugh, 41, 121

Bonner, Herbert, 45
Borrowing money, 76, 83
Boston, 25, 26; *see also* Levin, Murray B.; Bruner, Jerome S.
Brown, Edmund (Pat), 9, 13, 22, 42, 45, 77, 122
Bruner, Jerome S., 24, 25, 26
Buchanan, William, 16, 74
Bullitt, Stimson, 100, 110
Bumper stickers, 76
Burdick, Eugene, 15
Burke, 60, 115
Business groups, 62, 63, 70
political training programs of, 63

California, advantages of incumbents, 126
delegates to national conventions, 79
expensiveness of campaigns, 75
1962 election, 9
political history, 6-9
California Democratic Council, 8, 9, 17, 20, 37, 43, 44, 92, 124, 125
contribution of workers, 43
membership of, 44
in primary elections, 35
California Progressives, The, 6
California Republican Assembly, 9, 20, 43
California, University of, 27
Campaign Decision-makers, 58
Campaign management firms, 87
cost of, 88
Campaign managers, 53, 88
Campaign schools, *see* National committees (of political parties), training schools
Campbell, Angus, 2, 24, 61, 90
Candidacy, 14–31
for two offices, 133
Candidate-recruiting committees, 17–19
in Eleventh District in 1952, 18
Candidates, appeals based on, 113–115
attractive characteristics, develop-

141

ment of, 15
characteristics of, Bay Area, 27–31
characteristics preferred by voters, 23–26
experienced, 22–23, 60, 110, 115, 123
factors considered by, 20–23
group memberships, 72
importance as a campaign resource, in general elections, 14
in primary elections, 33
incomes, 28
loss of, while campaigning, 81
inexperienced, 22–23, 60, 110, 115, 123
list of Bay Area, 135
localism of, 128
number of campaign days, 103
of potential, 18–19
occupations, 30
residence in California, length of, 28
Cannon, James M., 24
Cantando, Leonard, 135
Cantril, Hadley, 25, 64, 113
Capitalism, Socialism and Democracy, see Schumpeter, Joseph
Catholics, 53, 61
CDC, *see* California Democratic Council
Central committees, 98; *see also* County central committees
Chamber of Commerce, 63
Charles, Ron, 135
Chicago, 4
Christenson, Reo M., 64
Church groups, 63, 64
Citizen clubs, 45
City councilmen, 66
Civic clubs, 64, 72
Civil rights, 116
Clapp, Charles L., 20, 41, 56, 64, 74, 75, 77, 106
Clausen, Donald, 135
Cohelan, Jeffery, 135
Colleges attended by candidates, 27
Committee on Political Education (AFL-CIO), 62, 63, 64, 67; *see also* Labor unions

Community Political Systems, 86
Compactness of districts, 131
Competitive candidates, *see* Competitiveness
Competitiveness, activities, 106
appeals, based on issues, 117
content and volume of, 121
Bay Area districts, 122, 135–136
candidates, characteristics, 29–30
number of, 22
citizen participation, 120
concept to substitute for compactness of district, 131
days, number of campaign, 103
definition, 4
endorsements by national leaders, 40
factors considered by candidates, 21
financial contributions from national committees, 41
fund raising chairman, 83
groups, support by, 67, 72
measures of, used by party leaders, 39
money, amounts and sources of, 80
professional public opinion polls, use of, 54
role of parties in promoting, 122
search for information, on content of issues, 59
on voter opinions, 60
unfair appeals, 119
voter turnout, 121
workers, characteristics of, 93
collection of money by, 84
number of, 91
replacement of, 98
sources of, 92–93
Compleat Politician, The: Political Strategy in Massachusetts, 24, 26
Condon, Robert, 130
Congressional campaign committees, *see* National committees (of political parties)
Congressional district campaign committees, 41, 42

Congressional pay increase, 55
Congressional polls, see Polls, public opinion; Polls, congressional
Congressional Quarterly Almanac, 34, 62, 127
Congressional Quarterly Weekly Report, 20, 58, 63, 76, 78, 82
Congressional Record, 58
Congressional session, length of, 10, 40, 103, 108
Congressman, The: His Work As He Sees It, see Clapp, Charles L.
Contractors, 62
Contributors, financial, geographical location, 78, 83
 in primary elections, 36
 wealthy, 82
Converse, Philip E., 2, 24, 61, 90
Cookbooks for brides, 110
Costantini, Edmond, 79
Costs of Democracy, The, see Heard, Alexander
Cotter, Cornelius P., 41
County central committees, 13, 45, 92
 candidate disappointment with, 42–43
 in primary elections, 35
CRA, see California Republican Assembly
Cross-filing, 6, 8, 125
Cuban missile crisis, 10, 40, 116, 127
Cummings, Milton, 126
Cutright, Phillips, 86, 106

Dahl, Robert A., 90
Danner, Bryant, 58
Data sources, 4
Day, typical campaign, 108
Days spent campaigning, number of, 103
Debates, 56, 57
Democracy, definition, 1
 implications of findings for, 120–133
Democratic candidates, see Party, political (Democratic versus Republican)
Democratic Congressional Campaign Committee, 57, 74; see also National committees (of political parties)
Democratic Leadership Corps in California, The, 79
Democratic National Committee, 45; see also National committees (of political parties)
Democratic Senate Campaign Committee, 67; see also National committees (of political parties)
Detroit, 26
DeVany, Philip M., 49
Devine, Dan, 26
Dexter, Lewis A., 24, 60
Doctors, see Medical groups
Donovan, Joseph, 136
Douglas, Helen Gahagan, 117
Dreyer, Edward C., 54

East Bay (Berkeley-Oakland), 13, 84
Economic effects, on candidate, of campaigning, 22–23
Education of candidates, 28
Edwards, W. Donlon, 136
Eldersveld, Samuel J., 86, 90
Election campaign, definition, 1
Eleventh District, candidate recruiting committee in 1952, 18; see also San Mateo county
Eulau, Heinz, 16
Experience, 24, 30; see also Candidates, experienced
Experienced candidates, see Candidates, experienced

Factory gates, 72, 108
Family picture, 113, 115
Farm Bureau, 63, 70
Farm groups, 63
Farmers Union, 63
Federal Communications Commission, 50
Federation of Republican Women, 43, 92
Ferguson, Jenniellen W., 9
Ferguson, LeRoy C., 16

Field secretaries, 88
Finance committees, 81
Finances, *see* Money
Financial statements of candidates, 74
FM radio stations, 50
480, The, 15
Fourteenth District, campaign in, 123
Fourth District, 44
  description of campaign, 11–12
  recruitment process for Democratic candidate, 17
  see also Leggett, Robert; Honsinger, L. V. (Mike)
Francis amendment (ballot proposition 24), 9
Franking privilege, 76, 109, 131
Freeman, Howard E., 64
Friends of candidate, as basis for group support, 68
  money from, 82
  as source of workers, 92
Funds, campaign, *see* Money

Georgia, 6
Gerrymandering, prevention of, 131
Goldberg, Dorothy P., 19, 20, 21
Goldwater, Barry, 78, 116
Government employees groups, 63
Groups, 61–73
  appeals based on, 118
  in Fourteenth District, 125
  high political participation in San Francisco, 65
  importance as a campaign resource, in general elections, 14
  in primary elections, 33
  money contributed, 81
  participants in candidate-recruiting process, 15, 16–17
  patterns of support, 69–73
  primary elections, 35
  public awareness of, 63
  resources needed to secure support of, 66–68
  techniques for securing support of, 65–69
  value of particular, 62–65

Gubser, Charles, 136

Hacker, Andrew, 63
Halleck, Charles, 114
Harris, Louis, 52
Hathorn, Guy B., 41
Havemann, Ernest, 24
Headquarters, campaign, 131
Health of candidates, 23
Heard, Alexander, 70, 74, 83, 101, 106
Hearings on Legislative Branch Appropriations for 1968, 50, 109
Hennessy, Bernard C., 41
Hodges, Luther, 11
Hoffman, Paul J., 9
Honsinger, L. V. "Mike", 11, 22, 72, 76, 79, 95, 115, 135
Humphrey, Hubert, 10

Ichord, Richard, 26
Income, of candidates, 28
  loss of, while campaigning, 81
Incumbency, activities, 107
  advantages in securing resources, 122–123
  appeals, based on candidate, 113
    based on groups, 118
    based on issues, 117
  appeals, campaign, 112
  auxiliary groups, support from, 43
  campaign managers, 88
  candidates, characteristics of, 29
    factors considered by, 23
  classification of Bay Area candidates, 135–136
  county central committees, attitude toward, 43
  days, number of campaign, 103
  experience, 26–27
  group support, 70–71
  groups, statements before, 66
  mailings, 109
  money, amounts and sources of, 80
    collection of, by workers, 84
    mail appeals for, 84
    needed, 75–76
    raised, 77

146 *Index*

dent, 40
Letters to congressmen, *see* Mail
Leuthold, David A., 6, 16, 24, 75, 90
Levin, Murray B., 24, 25, 26
Library of Congress, 56, 131
Liquor, 63
Literary Digest, 52
Living expenses, hidden, 79
Localism of candidates, 128
Los Angeles Dodgers, 10
Lowrey, Lloyd, 11, 17

Machines, use of, 86
Machinists, International Association of, 63
Mail appeals for funds, 84
Mail, as source of information on voter opinions, 49
  and age of congressmen, 60
Mailings to voters, 45, 46, 109
Mailliard, William, 12, 13, 44, 82, 83, 114, 130, 135
Marcantonio, Vito, 117
Marvick, Dwaine, 83, 94, 102
Massachusetts, 26; *see also* Boston; Levin, Murray B.; and Bruner, Jerome
Masters, Nicholas, 63, 67
Mayo, Charles G., 16
McCaffree, Floyd, 41
McPhee, William N., 64, 103
Meals, fund-raising, 84
Medical groups, 35–36, 63, 70
Medicare, 51, 116
Men, voter preferences for, 25
Merchants, 64
Military service of candidates, 27
Miller, Clem, 18, 135
Miller, George P., 135
Miller, Warren E., 2, 24, 61, 90, 113
Missouri, legislators, 126
  University of, 26
Money, 39, 74–85
  amount, available in 1958, 1960 and 1962, 77
  needed, 74
  amounts raised, 77–78
  borrowing, 76, 83
  California campaigns, greater expense of, 75
  in Fourteenth District, 124
  friends, from, 82
  geographical location of contributors, 78
  groups, from, 69, 81
  hidden living expenses, 81
  loss of income while campaigning, 81
  mail appeals for, 84
  meals, fund-raising, 84
  out-of-district contributors, 83
  primary elections, 35–36
  procedures for acquiring, 83–85
  purposes for which spent, 101
  recontributions, 82
  sources of, 78–83
  timeliness of contributions, 76
  waste of, 75
  wealthy contributors, from, 82
  workers, contributions by, 79
Mowry, George E., 6
Murphy, 26

Name Candidates in Detroit Elections, 26
Name identification of Congressmen, 26, 113
Names, well-known, 26
National Association of Manufacturers, 62
National committees (of political parties), 40
  financial contributions, of, 41
  information about issues, 57
  research assistance by, 41
  timeliness of contributions, 76
  training schools, 41, 57–58, 59, 132
  see also Democratic Congressional Campaign Committee; Democratic National Committee; Democratic Senate Campaign Committee; Republican Congressional Campaign Committee; Republican National Campaign Committee
National Education Association, 63
New Mexico, *see* Judah, Charles
New York, 78
New York Yankees, 10

Newsletters, congressional, 95; *see also* Franking privilege; Mailings to voters
Newspapers, 7, 13, 35–36, 64
 process of decision-making, 69
 support for likely winners, 68
Ninth Wave, The, 15
Nixon, Charles, 83, 94, 102
Nixon, Richard, 9, 78, 117
Nominations, long term, 133
Non-incumbents, see incumbency

Oakland Tribune, The, 68
Occupations, Bay Area candidates, 30
O'Connell, John, 12, 13, 40, 45, 69, 70, 82, 83, 97, 117, 135
Office staff, congressional, as campaign assistants, 76
Official Manuals, State of Missouri, 126
Olson, David M., 15, 19, 20, 21, 106
Opponents, former, support by, 45, 119
Opposite party support, 44
Orange County, 97
Oregon, 5; *see also* Seligman, Lester
Out-of-district contributors, 83
Owens, John R., 74

Participation in campaigns, 120
Party and Representation: Legislative Politics in Pennsylvania, see Sorauf, Frank
Party Committees and National Politics, 41
Party leaders, 22, 38–46
 appeals based on, 115
 auxiliary organizations, 43–44
 definition, 38
 denials of support by, 39–40
 national, 40–41
 official state and local, 41–42
 primary elections, 35
 role in recruiting candidates, 15, 19
Party, political (Democratic versus Republican), activities, campaign, 103
 appeals, based on candidate, 115
  based on groups, 118
  based on issues, 116
  based on party, 115
 appeals, campaign, 112
 auxiliary organizations, assistance from, 43
 campaign management firms, use of, 87
 candidates, characteristics of, 29
 classification of Bay Area candidates, 135
 competitive, efforts to be, 106
 congressional polls, satisfaction with, 60
 county central committees, 42
 days, number of campaign, 103
 endorsements by national leaders, 40
 fund-raising meals, 84
 group support, acquisition of, 72
 groups from which received support, 70
 mail received, 50
 money, amounts and sources of, 79
  collection of, by workers, 84
  from groups, 81
  from wealthy people, 82
 national committees, financial contributions from, 41
 precinct organizations, 42, 91, 106
 professional public opinion polls, use of, 54
 search for information on content of issues, 58, 59
 statewide candidates, relation with, 42
 voters, characteristics of, 103
 workers, characteristics of, 93
  financial contributions by, 79
  number of, 91
  political orientation of, 94, 96, 116
  sources of, 92–93
Party splits, 44
Party support, 32–47
 importance as a campaign resource
  in general elections, 14
  in primary elections, 33

148　Index

Patronage, 98
Peace groups, 13, 35–36, 66, 69, 70, 116
Pennsylvania, *see* Sorauf, Frank
Personal contact, as source of information on voter opinions, 50–51
  as means of influencing voters, 106
Personal friends of candidates, 25
Petersen, Harold, 135
Petersen, Svend, 8
Peterson, Arthur L., 41
Petroleum industry, 63
Pitchell, Robert J., 87
Pledge cards, 97, 124
Political Decision-makers, see Marvick, Dwaine
Political Life: Why People Get Involved in Politics, see Lane, Robert
Political Opinion and Electoral Behavior: Essays and Studies, 54
Political Parties: A Behavioral Analysis, 90
Politics in America, 1945–64, 126, 127
Politics of Nonpartisanship, The: A Study of California City Elections, 64
Politics, Parties and Pressure Groups, 3, 112
Politics U.S.A.: A Practical Guide to the Winning of Public Office, 24
Politics Without Power: The National Party Committees, 41
Polls, public opinion, 51–55
  congressional, 54–55, 60, 109
  by Bay Area congressmen, 54–55
  professional, 51–54
    definition, 52
    use of, by campaign managers, 53
Polsby, Nelson W., 112
Postal clerks, 71
  National Federation of Postal Clerks, 63
Precinct organizations, 42, 91, 106

Precinct workers, effect of, 86
  telephoning as means of recruiting, 97
Preprimary Endorsements in California Politics, 44
Presidential elections, effect on fund raising, 77, 128
Presidential Elections: Strategies of American Electoral Politics, 112
President's Commission on Campaign Costs, 75
Primary elections, 32–38
  competitiveness of, compared to general elections, 34–35
  public interest in, 37
  voter preferences in, 32–33
Professional polls, *see* Polls, public opinion, professional
Professional Public Relations and Political Power, 87
Professional workers, *see* Workers, professional
Progressives (political party), 6–8
Protestant church groups, 63
Public Opinion 1935–1946, see Cantril, Hadley
Purchases of group endorsements, 65–66

Ramsey, Maurice M., 26
Ranney, Austin, 33
Reapportionment, 10, 34, 128, 130
Reasons for running, *see* Candidates, factors considered by
Recontributions, financial, 82
Recruitment of Candidates from Bernalillo County to New Mexico of Representatives, 1956, The, see Judah, Charles B.
Recruits, 15
Reelection success, 126
Reporter, The, 109
Representation, style of, 114–115
Republican candidates, *see* Party, political (Democratic versus Republican)
Republican Congressional Campaign Committee, 41; *see also* Na-

Index **149**

tional committees (of political parties)
Republican National Campaign Committee, 67; *see also* National committees (of political parties)
Republican Women's Club, *see* Federation of Republican Women
Requests, for group support, 66, 71
for money, 83
for party leader support, 39
Residence in California, length of, by candidates, 28
Residency requirements, 133
Resources, campaign, 2
relative importance as indicated by voter responses, 14
Richards, Richard, 9
Riggs, Robert E., 24, 26
Role of the Federal Government scale, 37, 96
Roper, Elmo, 90
Roosevelt, 26
Roosevelt, Franklin D., 52
Rosenbaum, Walter A., 54
Rosenzweig, Robert M., 20
Rossi, Peter H., 86, 106
Rousselot, John, 117
Rowe, Leonard, 16, 44, 74, 75
Rusk, Dean, 45

Salaries for candidates, 132
Samish, Artie, 8
Sandmire, James, 92
San Francisco, high political participation by groups in, 65
purchase of group endorsements, 65
source of wealthy contributors, 78
San Francisco Bay Area, 5-8
economic characteristics, 6
demographic characteristics, 6
1962 elections, 10-13
political history, 6-9
San Francisco Giants, 10
San Mateo county, as source of wealthy contributors, 78; *see also* Eleventh District
Savings and loan industry, 63

Scammon, Richard M., 34
Schumpeter, Joseph A., 1, 120
Scoble, Harry, 67, 70
Self-starters, 15
definitions of, 16
Seligman, Lester, 16, 19
Senators, reelection success of, 126
Seniority, 114
Shelley, John, 135
Showel, Morris, 64
Sinclair, Upton, 7
Sixth District, description of campaign, 12-13
securing of opposite party support, 44-45
see also Mailliard, William; O'Connell, John
Snowiss, Leo M., 4
Sorauf, Frank, 15, 16, 19, 20, 21
Speeches, 109
Split-ticket giving, 83
SRC, *see* Survey Research Center, University of Michigan
Stanford University, 27
Statewide candidates, 9, 42
effect on fund raising, 77
Statistical History of the American Presidential Elections, A, 8
Stokes, Donald E., 2, 24, 61, 90, 113
Strategy, campaign, 53
definition, 3
Superintendent of Public Instruction, 9
Sure losers, *see* Competitiveness
Sure winners, *see* Competitiveness
Survey of campaign workers, methodology, 90
questionnaire, 137-140
Survey Research Center, University of Michigan, 2
1952 survey, 92
1960 survey, 14, 25, 64
1962 survey, 14, 94
1964 survey, 33
see also Campbell, Angus; Converse, Philip E.; Miller, Warren E.; and Stokes, Donald E.

Teamsters Union, 63, 64

Index

Telephone bill, 81
Telephoning as a means of securing precinct workers, 97
Texas, *see* Olson, David M.
Third parties, support for, 8
Thurber, James P., Jr., 136
Timeliness of financial contributions, 76
Training schools, *see* National committees (of political parties), training schools; *see also* Business groups, political training programs of.
Trends, national, effect on congressional reelection, 130
Truman, Harry, 112
Two-year congressional term, 128

Unfair appeals, 118
Unions, labor, *see* Labor unions
United Auto Workers of America, 63
United Republican Finance Committees, 42, 78
United Steel Workers of America, 63
Utilities, public, 63

Veterans groups, 63
Veterans of Foreign Wars, 63
Virginia, 6
Voekel, John, 34
Voter registration, by party, by district, 22, 46
Voter turnout, 121
Voters preferences in candidate characteristics, *see* Candidates, characteristics preferred by voters
Voting: A Study of Opinion Formation in a Presidential Campaign, see Berelson, Bernard R.

Wahlke, John C., 16, 20
Warren, Earl, 8, 12
Waste of money, 75
Weidner, Charles, 124, 128, 132, 136
Weidner, Edward, 125
West Virginia, 6

What It Means To Be A Politician, 100
Whitaker and Baxter, 87
Whitaker, Clem, 100
White, John P., 74
Who Governs?, 90
Wilcox, Walter, 54, 60
Wildavsky, Aaron B., 112
Wisconsin, 6, 32
Wolfinger, Raymond E., 86
Woodward, Julian L., 90
Workers, 86–99
  activities of, 102
  amateur, 89–98
    definition of, 89
  attitudes toward candidates, 95
  auxiliary organizations, from, 43
  characteristics, 92
  financial contributions of, 79
  groups, provided by, 69
  incentives offered to, 97
  in Fourteenth District, 125
  money, collecting, 83
  number of, 90
  political orientation, 93, 116
  opposite party, from, 46
  primary election, characteristics of, 37
  professional, 87–89
    definition of, 87
  replacement of, 98
  sources of, 92–93
  survey of, methodology, 90
    questionnaire, 137–140
  techniques of recruiting, 96–98
  voter turnout, 121
Working people, 72
World Series, 10
"Written-off" candidates, 39
Wyant, Rowena, 49

Yemen, 57
Young Democrats, 43
Young Republicans, 43
Younger, Arthur, 136

Zon, Mary G., 70